Kingdom Stories

Kingdom Stories

Telling, Leading, Discerning

Vaughan S. Roberts

scm press

© Vaughan S. Roberts 2020

Published in 2020 by SCM Press
Editorial office
3rd Floor, Invicta House,
108–114 Golden Lane,
London EC1Y 0TG, UK
www.scmpress.co.uk

SCM Press is an imprint of Hymns Ancient & Modern Ltd
(a registered charity)

H
Y
M Ancient
N &Modern;
S

Hymns Ancient & Modern® is a registered trademark of
Hymns Ancient & Modern Ltd
13a Hellesdon Park Road, Norwich,
Norfolk NR6 5DR, UK

978-0-334-05902-8

British Library Cataloguing in Publication data
A catalogue record for this book is available
from the British Library

Typeset by Regent Typesetting
Printed and bound by
CPI Group (UK) Ltd

The Kingdom is present already,
mingling disguised with the untransformed
and common life.

Evelyn Underhill, *Abba: Meditations on
the Lord's Prayer*, 1940, p. 38

Contents

Acknowledgements   ix
Foreword by the Rt Revd Dr Christopher Cocksworth   xi
Introduction   xiii

1 **Kingdom Stories**   1

   1 Introduction   1
   2 Storytelling   3
   3 Jesus and the kingdom   4
   4 A sculpted kingdom story   10
   5 A poetic kingdom story   12
   6 A cinematic kingdom story   14
   7 Churches and kingdom stories   16
   8 Kingdom stories: a preliminary summary   18

2 **Jesus and Kingdom Stories**   21

   1 Introduction   21
   2 Kingdom stories and risk
     (*Jesus' temptations*)   23
   3 Kingdom stories and followership
     (*The calling of the disciples*) 30
   4 Kingdom stories and typologies
     (*Parable of the farmer and the seed*) 39
   5 Kingdom stories and authenticity
     (*Who do you say that I am?*)   46

6 Kingdom stories and purpose
  (*The cost of building a tower and going to war*)   52
7 Kingdom stories, wisdom and meaning
  (*Let anyone with ears listen*)   58
8 Kingdom stories and discipleship
  (*Parable of the talents*)   65
9 Kingdom stories and trust
  (*Jesus washes the disciples' feet*)   72
10 Jesus and kingdom stories: conclusion   80

3 **The Church and Kingdom Stories**   83

  1 Introduction   83
  2 End of times and engaged eschatology   85
  3 End of life and engaged eschatology   93
  4 The Church and kingdom stories: conclusion   97

4 **One Kingdom Story in Detail**   102

  1 Introduction   102
  2 What was the story?   104
  3 What were the outcomes?   106
  4 Why did this happen?   107
  5 What are the implications for ministry and story?   108
  6 One kingdom story in detail: conclusion   129

Conclusion: Storying the Kingdom   132

  1 A kingdom story   132
  2 How do we identify kingdom stories?   136
  3 Kingdom stories: telling, leading, discerning   143

Afterword by the Rt Revd Professor Christopher
  Herbert   144
Bibliography and Further Reading   146
Index of Biblical References   153
Index of Names and Subjects   155

Acknowledgements

I have always been interested in stories, in how they work as forms of art, as well as how they engage people and organizations, so this project has deep roots. I am grateful to Chris Herbert who was – in Anglican terminology – my training incumbent who not only shared this enthusiasm but encouraged it and has generously written an afterword for this volume. I am indebted to Professor Iain L. Mangham and others at the University of Bath's School of Management who enabled me to take this interest and turn it into an action research PhD on organizational storytelling in church communities.

My gratitude also extends to my friend Professor David Sims who has co-operated with me in much organizational storytelling over the years and kindly collaborated on our book *Leading by Story: Rethinking Church Leadership* (2017), which forms the foundation for much that follows here.

Parts of this volume have been shared with others. I am grateful to the Bishop of Coventry, Christopher Cocksworth, for his invitation to lead the Coventry Diocese ordination retreat in 2019 and for writing a foreword to this book. Some of the ideas in Chapter 2 were offered to those preparing to be ordained deacons and priests, and I am grateful for their feedback, comments and questions. I am also deeply thankful to Naomi Nixon, Alex Williams, Richard Cooke and the Diocesan Training Partnership for all their hard work that went into making the retreat so enjoyable, and their support for my sabbatical visit to Orvieto and Assisi.

Some of the thinking in Chapter 4 has been presented to the Bishop of Barking, Peter Hill, and his leadership team during a residential at the Royal Foundation of St Katherine; with the British Sociological Association Sociology of Religion Study Group conference at the University of Cardiff, and the Theology, Religion and Popular Culture Network conference at the University of Kent. I greatly appreciate the opportunities to discuss my ideas with those attending three such stimulating events.

In addition, it is right and proper to acknowledge the hard work of all those who were involved in the Warwick Poppies 2018, including the organizing committee (David and Gill Benson, David and Gail Guest, Helen and Tony Fitzpatrick, Carol and Richard Warren), the churchwardens (John Luxton and Gail Guest), St Mary's church office (Felicity Bostock and Glynis Nixon), Doreen Mills, Kirsteen Robson and all who created the prayer trail, and the wider community of St Mary's, Warwick, who shared in the project's joys and frustrations, and all who contributed to the creation of 65,000 knitted poppies.

I am very grateful to David Shervington and the team at SCM Press for their support, diligence and hard work in bringing this book to fruition. And to Kirsteen Robson who commented critically and helpfully on an early draft of the manuscript.

As ever with a book such as this, close family are also a crucial part of the story even though they have little choice in the matter. The love and good humour of the Leyton family (Becky, Chris, Elijah, Noah and Emilia) and the Roberts family (Jon, Soph and Luna) have been so important to me along the way; as has the enduring love and patience of my wife Mandy.

Foreword

by the Rt Revd Christopher Cocksworth

'The kingdom of heaven is like ...', said Jesus as he began to tell a story. For generations the Church has repeated those stories as it has retold the story of Jesus, setting Jesus and his story in the context of Israel and its story – the story of God creating the world, coming to the world and consummating God's purposes of love for the world.

Christian faith is defined by a narrative. It is a grand, over-arching story that sweeps through time and space, making great claims about all that is and ever has been and ever will be. It is also an intensely personal story that, for all its cosmic breadth, touches individuals, families and communities in their locality and ordinary life. We see it in John's Gospel within its first chapter. One moment we are hearing about the Word who was God and through whom all things came into being. The next we are hearing words spoken by this Word now made flesh, asking two people, 'What are you looking for?'

Vaughan S. Roberts, priest and theologian, organizational theorist and church leader, inhabits this big story and observes the way people are caught up into it and can find their meaning through it. Through close attention to the experiences of every-day life, especially common life in organizations and churches, Vaughan is skilled at hearing stories and then retelling those stories within the story of God's abiding interest and involve-ment in the world. In so doing, eyes and ears are opened to the deep significance of human experience as an arena of the activity of God.

Vaughan is Vicar of what is effectively the county church of Warwickshire, and Team Rector of all the parishes in that historic town. It would be easy to become totally absorbed in the round of busyness that such a ministry requires. Vaughan knows, though, that to serve the community to which he was – as you will read later – strongly pulled by the gentle call of God, he needs to find time to think and to reflect, to read and to discern. The fruit of that sort of careful reflection is to be seen in the pages that follow. Drawing on biblical scholarship, on studies of business organization and leadership, on art, literature and music, Vaughan brings us close to Jesus the storyteller and, in the manner of Jesus, helps us to see God at work in everyday life.

Readers will be able to see why I invited Vaughan to lead our diocesan ordination retreat in 2019. I wanted these soon-to-be-ordained deacons and priests to be inspired *to read* – to read Scripture, to read books of theology and other disciplines, to read the arts in all their forms, in order that they might learn to read better the work of God in the different situations into which they would be sent throughout their ministries. I am grateful to Vaughan for rising to that request and providing that for which I had hoped; and I am delighted that his beautifully constructed retreat addresses have been expanded into this engaging book. *Kingdom Stories* gives not only the theory of why story is so important in human life and Christian ministry but also provides worked examples – especially the phenomenon of the Warwick Poppies – of how to tell the story of God at work in lives and localities. It has much to teach us all about how our own stories are part of a bigger story, a story – to return to the story of Jesus as told in John's Gospel – of 'grace and truth'.

The Rt Revd Christopher Cocksworth
Bishop of Coventry and Chair of the Church of England's Faith and Order Commission

Introduction

A kingdom story

It had been a very long day and everyone felt tired and exhausted. I was sitting outside the local lakeside tavern with Bartholomew, sharing a carafe of wine. Peter and Andrew were trying to talk one of the local fishermen into lending them his boat. He was always doing that, Peter. Whenever something dramatic happened and he wasn't sure how to cope, he'd go back to something that was familiar. The times he'd say, 'Right, I'm going fishing!' and then go off in search of a boat, daring the rest of us not to follow him, were beyond number. I can't really remember what the others were doing. Judas was probably checking the money. That was always something I never understood. Jesus had plenty of people around him who could have looked after the money – Matthew for one! And yet he chose Judas. In my opinion, either Jesus was a terrible judge of character or far too trusting.

Anyway, Bartholomew and I were having a quiet drink outside Judith's tavern as the day drew to a quiet close. We'd talked a little about Peter's outburst, 'You are the Christ of God', and what we took to be Jesus' rather unassuming acceptance of such a momentous title. But it was always difficult to pin him down on that matter.

I was just saying that there hadn't been a really good drop of Galilean red wine for at least six years, and that we really should go and see Jesus' friend Lazarus more often because he always had a few choice wines set aside, when Bartholomew turned to me and said, 'I wonder what death really tastes like?' I must have had a dazed expression, because he repeated the question again. 'You know, Jesus told us that there were some standing there who would not taste death before they see the kingdom of God. And I just wonder what death *tastes* like?'

Now, admittedly it was often quite difficult to tune into Bartholomew's quirky observations on life but, even by his off-the-wall standards, this was an odd comment. I responded rather lamely, 'I don't think that was really the point Jesus was getting at ...'

'So what was he "getting at"?' Bartholomew responded before I'd finished.

'Well ...' I hesitated because I hadn't really been too sure myself. 'Well ... I think he was saying that something BIG was going to happen and it was going to happen pretty soon.' I was confident that I wasn't too far off the mark. But my true and fast theological arrow obviously flew straight past Bartholomew's target and landed in some distant tree because he just drained the last bit of red wine in his cup and filled it again. A silence hung over the two of us as, in the distance, I could hear Peter shouting to Andrew, 'Get that wretched sail up now, you idiot!' So much for forgiving my brother seventy times seven, I thought idly as I wondered what to say next to my pensive drinking partner. Eventually I felt compelled to break the deepening melancholy mood. 'So, what do you think he meant?' I asked.

He glanced up at me from under his eyebrows and responded, 'Well, you know how Jesus is always going round, eating and drinking with everyone?' I nodded. 'And you know how he's always going on about how you can't fast while the bride-groom's with you?' I nodded again. 'And now he's talking about going up to Jerusalem?' This time I just let him continue. 'I think the feast is coming to an end and the fast is about to begin. Then I was thinking about Job, how all his troubles started at a feast and how he ended up in sackcloth and ashes. I think ...' He lowered his voice. 'I think death is going to taste like ashes.' At that point I filled my cup once more.

A cough came through the open window. 'That's an interesting way of understanding my words', said Jesus, putting his own cup on the window ledge and leaning out into the cooling dusk. 'I have to say, I didn't really see it like that.'

'Didn't you?' Bartholomew almost shouted. 'Would you mind telling us how you do see it, then? Because if we go up to Jerusalem, all I can see is suffering and disaster. They're not going to prepare a welcoming committee for us, you know!'

'I know that and you know that. Deep down, we all know what's waiting in Jerusalem. Why do you think Peter's gone fishing?' Jesus replied. His eyes sparkled for a moment. 'The shepherd wouldn't try to pull the wool over your eyes!' But Bartholomew was so embedded in his ashes he couldn't see an attempt at humour if it were floating in his wine goblet.

So Jesus continued, 'You're right. There's going to be no red carpet in the capital; no thanksgiving in the Temple and no pomp and circumstance from Pilate. We'll find sackcloth and ashes a plenty in Jerusalem ... and worse. That's the way of things. The journey through the wilderness was no picnic and the path of the prophets was strewn with thorns, so why should this be any different? But if it's ashes you're looking for in Jerusalem, then keep hold of those words in Isaiah: "provide for those who mourn in Zion – to give them a garland instead of ashes, the oil of gladness instead of mourning, the mantle of praise instead of a faint spirit" (Isaiah 61.3). We won't always be drinking wine like this, you know. It may not be quite as good as the stuff we get when we're with friends like Mary, Martha and Lazarus, but it's still much nicer than vinegar.' And I've wondered, since, how much he knew about what lay in store for him.

Jesus was about to turn away and go back to pick up his conversation with Judith and her companions. Then he hesitated. 'You may be right about one thing, Bartholomew. Death itself may taste like ashes, I'll grant you that. But what about the feast in the kingdom? I'd bet anything that the wine served then would make even Lazarus' taste like something from a herdsman's hip flask, but we ... I ... must drink from other cups first.' He sighed deeply and looked out into the distance, and the silence returned for a moment.

Then he tapped me on the shoulder and said, 'For goodness' sake, go and tell Peter he needs to be fishing from the other side of the boat. How many times do I have to tell him that?'

This approach of retelling stories to enter imaginatively into Jesus' life and teaching is used by many clergy and lay ministers to open up ideas about who Jesus was and the nature of the kingdom that he was proclaiming. The published works of Trevor Dennis (2003) and John Pritchard (2001) are good examples of this. But it is not only ministers who are fascinated by who Jesus was and what he represented. Sundry novelists have retold his story as well, from Charles Dickens and Dorothy L. Sayers to Philip Pullman and Anne Rice, together with numerous other writers of fiction.

Various historians have also taken this approach and a classic is Gerd Theissen's *The Shadow of the Galilean* (1987), which he describes as 'the quest of the historical Jesus in narrative form', and more recently Paula Gooder's *Phoebe: A Story* (2018), which is subtitled 'Pauline Christianity in narrative form'.

Some of this book's origins lie in such approaches to the Bible generally and the New Testament in particular. However, that is only part of my much more widespread interest in narrative and how all kinds of different stories are active in the lives of individuals and communities. In that respect, this volume relates to and draws together insights from practical theology, New Testament studies, Christianity and popular culture, organization and leadership studies.

Kingdom stories: telling, leading, discerning

My story about the conversation between Philip, Bartholomew and Jesus points us firmly towards the first two chapters of this book. There we shall examine the notion of God's kingdom and how that was proclaimed through Jesus' words and his actions such as sharing meals with those who were regarded as on the edge of respectable society, his understanding of Messiahship and the role of the Jerusalem Temple, his death on the cross and the nature of his sacrifice. We will be considering Mark's version of this story in Chapter 2.5.

Thus, Chapter 1 explores the background to the kingdom of God in Jesus' life and how historians have attempted to understand his eschatological proclamation. We shall briefly examine four approaches to eschatology: (i) imminent or apocalyptic eschatology, (ii) realized eschatology, (iii) inaugurated eschatology, and (iv) restoration eschatology. I will then use three stories from the artistic worlds of sculpture, poetry and cinema to discuss what I call an 'engaged' eschatology and what that might look like.

The second chapter takes this a stage further by bringing together some of Jesus' words and actions about God's kingdom, along with various challenges in contemporary ministry. We will consider eight stories about Jesus and the kingdom drawn from the four Gospels and put each of them alongside a term that relates it to our current context – risk, followership, typologies, authenticity, purpose, wisdom and meaning, discipleship, trust. In this way, we see how Jesus' eschatological world can engage with narratives found in today's churches.

In *Leading by Story*, David Sims and I argued that leading is better seen as a verb than a noun and I shall continue with that approach in this volume. Having said that, leadership exists as an entity in the minds of many and in the literature about how to lead, and as such it cannot be wished away. There will be times in what follows when we shall have to address this frequently used (and misused) concept. Nevertheless, we shall always be returning to storytelling and story-sharing as activities that unavoidably involve telling, leading and discerning.

One typical characteristic of eschatology is that it refers in some way to the end times, and Chapter 3 will investigate this more thoroughly. In particular, we shall explore the role of binary perceptions in shaping various understandings of 'the end', and once again we will bring together art, popular culture, theology and organization studies. First, we shall look at Luca Signorelli's depiction of the Last Judgement in his frescoes for Orvieto Cathedral and see how his artistic binary of heaven and earth relates to the dichotomy that is often drawn between leadership and management in modern thinking. Then we shall scrutinize Henry Scott Holland's 'poem' 'Death is Nothing at All' and how his original sermon reflects a binary between 'death is nothing at all' and death as 'the supreme irrevocable disaster'. Holland's eschatology will also engage with aspects of contemporary culture in the stories told in the films *The Shape of Water* and *Coco*.

Chapter 4 takes us back into the realm of practical ministry and engaged eschatology through the story of one church's project to commemorate the one hundredth anniversary of the conclusion of the First World War. Warwick Poppies 2018 set out to collect 11,610 knitted poppies to mark that anniversary and received over 65,000 poppies donated to the project. The church where the display was mounted usually has around 37,000 visitors per year but during the three months of the exhibition, 47,000 people visited. This chapter seeks to tease out what a narrative approach to this experience of remembrance, death and bereavement can teach us through (i) stories online, (ii) 'control' of stories, (iii) structuring of people's life stories, (iv) seeking transcendent (bigger) stories, (v) ending stories, and (vi) loss of stories, and how these relate to the wider concept of kingdom stories.

In my conclusion I will outline five ways in which we can recognize the kingdom stories that are told, led and discerned, but we turn, in the first instance, to explore the nature of kingdom stories and an engaged eschatology.

I

Kingdom Stories

1 Introduction

In the fantasy world of Westeros created in the novels by George R. R. Martin and dramatically brought to life in the TV series *Game of Thrones*, produced by David Benioff and D. B. Weiss, the person who rules over the Seven Kingdoms of Westeros sits upon the Iron Throne. This seat of governance has been created from the 1,000 swords of those who were defeated in the War of Conquest to unify the kingdoms. It is an image that visually and symbolically links monarchy and power. To sit upon the throne is to wield immense power, but to achieve possession of that symbol of kingship requires the holder to exercise single-minded domination and ruthless might.

Perhaps surprisingly, this connection between power and symbols of monarchy is also made in some Christian hymnody. One example is Francis Potts' opening verse for 'Angel voices ever singing'. Although the swords of Westeros have been replaced by angelic harps, the connection between God's throne and God's power is made clear in that verse's last line:

Angel voices ever singing
round Thy throne of light,
angel harps, forever ringing,
rest not day nor night;
thousands only live to bless Thee
and confess thee Lord of might.

Another instance of royal imagery and divine power is provided by Edward Perronet's so-called 'Coronation Hymn', 'All
hail the power of Jesus' name', where angels are portrayed
lying prone before the majesty of Christ:

> All hail the power of Jesus' name;
> Let angels prostrate fall;
> Bring forth the royal diadem,
> To crown him Lord of all.

Perronet's words have been rewritten a number of times, partly
because, as J. R. Watson has observed, 'The original text is
full of awkward phrases and coded references' (Watson, 2002,
p. 211). Yet despite that, the underlying metaphor remains
clear that Christ is enthroned in heaven and all creatures
should be humble before the king.

The phrases 'kingdom of God' and 'the kingdom of heaven'
are characteristic of Jesus' language. Most New Testament
historians agree that Jesus used such terms but what he meant
by them continues to be hotly debated. The complexity is well
put by Ruth Etchells in her discussion of biblical language
and metaphor: 'We experience Christ's own language of what
God is "like" most powerfully in the parables: the kingdom of
heaven is like ... landowners with tenants, girls with lamps,
the dividing of the flocks into sheep and goats, mustard seed,
a wedding feast ... Such language of "likeness" is heard by us
of course, not only against the background of Jesus' own contemporary world (and ours), but also against the background
of the Scriptures his own world used' (Etchells, 1998, p. 5).

In other words, understanding what Jesus meant by references to 'the kingdom' involves knowledge about: Jesus and
the social context of first-century Palestine; the religious setting
in which he lived, including the Jewish Scriptures that shaped
so much of that culture; our own context, which is at the same
time both so different yet also provides new means and tools
for analysing Jesus' environment and teaching.

It is important to be clear at the outset what this book is

and is not about. It is not a study of Jesus' teaching about the kingdom of God and is therefore not a volume of New Testament studies. Having said that, it aims to be informed by work in that field but it is not a 'deep dive' into topics such as the historical Jesus or the nature of eschatology. However, it does take seriously Jesus' language of the kingdom and seeks to explore how that continues to be relevant, as Etchells suggests, in our contemporary world.

2 Storytelling

To that end, I aim to build on the insights into the Church and organizational storytelling developed with David Sims in *Leading by Story* (2017) and in my own work, particularly in *The Power of Story to Change a Church* (2016) and 'Aquifer Analysis: Told and Untold Stories in Warwick Churches' for *Untold Stories in Organizations* (2014). David and I argue that human beings are innate storytellers and that that is one of the principal ways in which we make sense of our world and our experiences. Furthermore, the way in which organizations of all kinds (including churches) make sense of their ministry and mission is through the multiplicity of narratives that are told within and outside that organization. This has important implications for leading and leadership in all collective activity, whether that is businesses, charities, voluntary bodies, churches or other settings.

In this book I shall reflect on Jesus' teaching about the kingdom of God and explore what I am calling an 'engaged eschatology'. By that I mean Jesus was always looking for signs of God's kingdom while encouraging his disciples and listeners to do the same. Such glimpses of God's activity in people's lives and in the wider world are what I identify as 'kingdom stories'. In terms of practical ministry and theology, this is where we find God is active inside and outside churches, and this is where the Body of Christ needs to be engaged with the kingdom where it continues to be manifest.

In his book *God's Companions*, Sam Wells puts it in these terms:

> the life-giving, restoring, reconciling gifts of the kingdom appear like the first flowers of spring, budding all over God's good creation. The gift of imagination is not about the scarcity of the Church but about the abundance of God. The Church does not need to ponder morosely its own short-comings in order to explain the breadth of the kingdom: the gift of imagination beyond the Church is not because God so resented the Church but because God so loved the world ... The signs of the kingdom in the world are a constant chal-lenge to the Church to renew its practices and to keep its heart open to receiving new gifts from God. (Wells, 2006, p. 34)

But what manner of kingdom is being revealed? Is it about exercising power and might, or is it apparent in other forms? How can we understand Jesus' proclamation of God's kingdom, and to what was he referring? It is to these questions that I now turn.

3 Jesus and the kingdom

Terms and phrases come with a past and with 'baggage'. King-dom is one such word, as we have already seen. It can signify the use and abuse of power, which is why some theologians have tried other terms, such as 'the reign of God' or the 'domain of God', but in what follows I will stay with the expression 'kingdom of God'. There are two reasons for this. First, it is an image that Jesus used frequently to describe his mission. As E. P. Sanders observes:

> [Jesus] used the word 'kingdom' an overwhelming number of times in comparison with other terms, and it was forced to carry a very wide range of meaning ... 'Future' and 'present'

in the teaching of Jesus have constituted a worrisome problem because we cannot say clearly what is present – nor even what he precisely thought of as future, whether a new order or cosmic cataclysm. (Sanders, 1985, p. 152)

And he goes on to say: 'if Jesus truly expected God to act decisively in the future, we must also assume that this expectation dominated and controlled his activity and message and that the future event is what primarily defines Jesus' view of "the kingdom"' (p. 154).

The second reason is that 'kingdom' does not have to automatically refer to an abusive relationship involving power and dominion. As the idea of kingdom stories is developed in what follows, it will become clear that they are not about authority and control but about identifying God's presence in our world. One New Testament historian notes how the German scholar Gustaf Dalman showed conclusively that in Jesus' teaching, God's kingdom refers primarily to divine activity in the world, and 'because this theme of God's action was so central to Jesus, the Kingdom of God has tended to become a cover-phrase for varied understandings of that action in the world' (Barbour, 2000, p. 370).

Commentators have set out many different ways in which they perceive Jesus to have understood the coming of God's kingdom or, to use the more technical term, eschatology. This kingdom typology sets out four distinct ways in which historians have framed Jesus' teaching and identifies one particular scholar with each form. However, it is important to keep in mind that not only is there great diversity and debate between and under each heading, but also there are other headings in addition to these four.

1 *Imminent or apocalyptic eschatology* (Albert Schweitzer). Jesus expected the imminent arrival of the kingdom of God and was heroically wrong in this belief. Schweitzer puts it in these terms:

the coming of the Kingdom of God is not only symbolically or analogically, but also really and temporally connected with the harvest. The harvest ripening on earth is the last! With it comes also the Kingdom of God which brings in the new age. When the reapers are sent into the fields, the Lord in Heaven will cause His harvest to be reaped by the holy angels. (Schweitzer, 1954, p. 355)

Even though Jesus was mistaken and the angels did not come to reap the harvest, Schweitzer believed we needed more people like Jesus who embraced the kingdom of God and was strengthened in his mission by that faith. As Schwarz has noted: 'It is relatively unimportant for Schweitzer that Jesus was actually deceived in his eschatological expectations. All-decisive is his attitude towards history and towards the obstacles he had to overcome in accomplishing his goal' (Schwarz, 2000, p. 133).

2 *Realized eschatology* (C. H. Dodd). The kingdom of God has arrived in and through Jesus' actions and ministry. Dodd puts it in this way:

> Jesus proclaims that the Kingdom of God has come, and He also foretells suffering and death for Himself and disasters upon Israel ... In rejecting Him, the Jewish nation rejected the Kingdom of God ... In weal or woe, the Kingdom of God had come upon them. (Dodd, 1961, pp. 58–9)

In Dodd's estimation, the kingdom has arrived with Jesus' resurrection and it returns whenever anyone experiences a new reality in Christ. One of my favourite illustrations of this perception of God's kingdom is a mural near to a church in Denver, Colorado (see Figure 1.1).

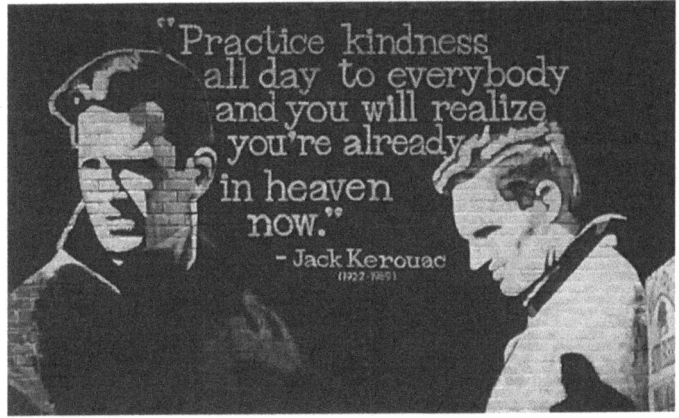

Figure 1.1: A contemporary expression of realized eschatology from a mural opposite the Cathedral Basilica of the Immaculate Conception, Denver, Colorado (photograph by Vaughan S. Roberts)

3 **Inaugurated eschatology** (Oscar Cullmann). The kingdom of God is inaugurated through Jesus but is yet to reach fulfilment. In this respect, the Easter experience of the risen Christ is fundamental:

> the new revelation imparted to the first Christians in that experience consisted in the realization that the present Lord is identical with the Jesus of Nazareth who appeared on earth and was crucified, and with the Son of Man who will one day come on the clouds of heaven. (Cullmann, 1963, p. 320)

Thus, the death and resurrection of Jesus become the mid-point of time, the kingdom has been inaugurated by these events and is waiting for its final fulfilment in a coming eschaton.

4 **Restoration eschatology** (E. P. Sanders). Here Jesus is seen as declaring the end of the present age and the dawn of a new one in the form of a restored covenant with YHWH. Sanders argues that there are

7

clear and undeniable indications that [Jesus] expected
the restoration *of Israel*; temple and twelve are national
symbols. In this context it is noteworthy that his message largely omits the typical *means* for the achievement
of restoration. That Jesus did not think that national
restoration would be achieved by arms is not especially
surprising. What is surprising is that, while looking for the
restoration of Israel, he did not follow the majority and
urge the traditional means towards that end: repentance
and a return to observance of the law. (Sanders, 1985,
p. 119 – emphasis original)

There is a sense in which Sanders' approach to Jesus and
his proclamation of God's kingdom is an updating of
Schweitzer's view, which takes on board a great deal of new
historical research.

As I say, this is not intended to be a comprehensive review of
scholarship across such a crowded field. There are numerous
other significant names whose work could and should be considered if that were the case.[1] Rather, my aim is to give a sense
of the range of views that exists about Jesus and the kingdom
of God and the challenges that need to be faced when writing
about this subject. The question of whether Jesus expected
God's kingdom to come on earth and – if so – in what form it
would arrive remains something that is keenly debated.

One area of common ground between most, if not all, New
Testament historians is that Jesus expected a coming tribu-
lation or crisis. As we can see, the nature of this anticipated and
fundamental change to the world continues to generate much
scholarship and further questions, which will not be resolved.
Where does that leave those of us involved in churches and
their ministry? If we take a step back and return to Dalman's
insight that, in speaking about the kingdom of God, Jesus is
identifying God's activity in the world, then we can begin to
see how the kingdom and contemporary ministry can connect.
This is where we turn to various notions of eschatology.

Richard Bauckham has succinctly defined eschatology as 'the story of the whole world and God's relationship with it from its creation to the end' (Bauckham, 2000, p. 206). In this book I shall employ what I am calling an 'engaged eschatology', and by that I mean Jesus encouraged his followers to look out for signs of God's kingdom or signs of God's activity in the world. What I am calling kingdom stories were one of his main means of conveying the nature of the crisis, where it was leading and what outcomes should be expected. Next I explore the concept of kingdom stories in more detail and the various ways in which they manifest themselves in our contemporary world.

One of the ways in which this happens is through the many forms of cultural expression that are inextricably bound up with meaning-making and storytelling. In his book *A Cultural Theology of Salvation*, Clive Marsh explores the connection between the doctrine of salvation, understanding God's kingdom and their relationship to the arts and popular culture. Marsh asks some relevant questions:

> how does what is being interpreted (religious text, painting, piece of music, TV programme) help us better discern and fashion human action in anticipating the kingdom of God which is yet to be? And how does our glimpse, hunch, or vision of what that kingdom of God is – the context in which God reigns – shape what we are articulating as a theological insight or statement? These are the key questions which drive theological hermeneutics. (Marsh, 2018, p. 42)

Let me outline three instances in which forms of popular culture offer glimpses of God's activity in the world through sculpture, poetry and film.

4 A sculpted kingdom story

This chapter began with a reference to the Iron Throne from the TV series *Game of Thrones* and how that acts as a symbol of power. Each first showing of an episode in the UK was followed by *Thronecast*, a fan-orientated discussion programme including interviews with the actors playing characters in the drama. The facsimile iron throne in that programme was created by sculptor Alfie Bradley, who has also made a 27-foot-tall statue of an angel consisting of confiscated blades involved in UK knife crimes.

The *Knife Angel* is a radical inversion or reinterpretation of knives and swords in people's lives and in society. It includes, on the wings, messages and stories from families and individuals affected by knife crime. Its creator says that this piece is not just a sculpture but involves the whole world around it.[2] The further he went on in the project, the more he became aware of how he was dealing with families and hearing their stories. Messages from those directly impacted could be engraved directly on to 'their' knife, and other messages were fed into the project through social media, all of which were on the angel's wings.

In April 2019, during Lent and over the Easter weekend, the *Knife Angel* (Figure 1.2) was displayed outside the rebuilt Coventry Cathedral, which had itself been the victim of violence during the Second World War, when it had been destroyed. The Cathedral's website included a message from Christopher Cocksworth, the Bishop of Coventry, which read:

> The Knife Angel is a stark reminder of a form of violent crime infecting our city and threatening lives with great danger, especially our young people. It also speaks the Coventry story – that weapons of hate and destruction can be re-worked into symbols of peace and hope, signalling a new future where violence is overcome. Together with people of every faith and none, we will not only care for the bereaved of such crimes but do all we can to build the sort of culture that eradicates

their causes. I'm really glad that the Knife Angel will stand near St Michael, the guardian angel and patron of Coventry's Cathedral.[3]

Figure 1.2: Alfie Bradley's Knife Angel *sculpture outside Coventry Cathedral, April 2019 (photograph by Vaughan S. Roberts)*

It is clear from the approach of the sculptor and the families, and the message from the Bishop, that the stories of people and communities are intimately bound up with this work of art. As well as names being added directly on to the sculpture itself, people brought photos, messages and flowers to lay beside the *Knife Angel* as they commemorated loved ones. This in itself is a form of kingdom story in terms of the shared narratives that are being woven together, as well as in the reworking of knives from symbols of power and dominion on the Iron Throne into an image of pain and a hope for the future that captures something of the essence of kingdom stories. Such a process of shared meaning-making involves a wholesale reimagining of something that we take for granted.

We shall return to the tragic issue of knife crime in Chapter 4.5 *(v) ending stories*, but in the meantime this characteristic of new insight or inversion of expectations is typical of kingdom stories and is a defining trait of engaged eschatology. Looking at another example from hymnody, the opening verse of Emily Elliott's popular reflection on the humility of Christ in taking human form upends metaphors of monarchy in the light of Jesus' incarnation:

> Thou didst leave Thy throne and Thy kingly crown,
> When Thou camest to earth for me;
> But in Bethlehem's home was there found no room
> For Thy holy nativity.
> O come to my heart, Lord Jesus,
> There is room in my heart for Thee.

The contrast between heaven and earth is mirrored by the idea that there was no room for Jesus and his family at the inn (Luke 2.7) but there is room in our hearts, and this is a theme that we can see clearly in our next kingdom story.

5 A poetic kingdom story

Another helpful way into understanding the nature of kingdom stories is through Francis Thompson's poem 'The Kingdom of God', which was among a number published after his early death from tuberculosis at the age of 48, after what Martin Warner calls his 'vagabond' life (Warner, 2009, p. 2). Thompson's verse is a reflection on the nature of God's kingdom and how we can glimpse it in our world:

> O world invisible, we view thee,
> O world intangible, we touch thee,
> O world unknowable, we know thee,
> Inapprehensible, we clutch thee!
>
> Does the fish soar to find the ocean,
> The eagle plunge to find the air –
> That we ask of the stars in motion
> If they have rumour of thee there?

Not where the wheeling systems darken,
And our benumbed conceiving soars! –
The drift of pinions, would we hearken,
Beats at our own clay-shuttered doors.

The angels keep their ancient places –
Turn but a stone and start a wing!
'Tis ye, 'tis your estrangèd faces,
That miss the many-splendoured thing.

But (when so sad thou canst not sadder)
Cry, – and upon thy so sore loss
Shall shine the traffic of Jacob's ladder
Pitched betwixt Heaven and Charing Cross.

Yea, in the night, my Soul, my daughter,
Cry, – clinging to Heaven by the hems;
And lo, Christ walking on the water,
Not of Genesareth, but Thames!

Thompson's poem has been anthologized on numerous occasions in recent times, including *The Poetry of Piety* by Ben Witherington III (a professor of New Testament studies) and Christopher Mead Armitage (a professor of English). In their analysis of this verse, Witherington and Armitage see Thompson urging readers to 'seek the God within rather than the God without'. For them the message of the poem is clear: 'God seeks us out where we live and speaks to us in a language or vision that we can grasp so that we need not miss "the many-splendoured thing" or its significance' (Witherington and Armitage, 2002, p. 121).

However, I would argue that it is important not to overplay the internal and underplay the external in Thompson's vision for the kingdom of God. The poet's references to Jacob's ladder (Genesis 28.10–19) and Christ walking upon the water (Mark 6.47–52 and parallels) suggest that God's actions from the past continue to be present now. Jacob's ladder can be found in Charing Cross and Christ walks upon the waters of the River Thames. An engaged eschatology will seek out stories and signs of God's kingdom wherever we are – whether that is Galilee, London or anywhere else. And when we spot glimpses or receive hunches about God's kingdom, we will inevitably write those into our personal stories and into the stories of the communities to which we belong. As Martin Warner states in his reflections on the 'yearning in our minds for the knowledge of God', which takes Thompson's poem as its starting point, 'poetry, art and music, the oblique sciences in the narrative of faith are indispensable for our demonstration of how we cross the barrier' (Warner, 2009, p. 42). We shall pick this up with the discussion about followership and another poem in Chapter 2.3.

6 A cinematic kingdom story

The process of seeking and finding visions of God's kingdom in and through the complexities of life experience is also manifest in many films. A recent example can be found in the movie *Lady Bird* (2017, dir. Greta Gerwig).

It is described on Wikipedia as a 'coming-of-age comedy-drama film',[4] which, up to a point, it is. However, I would argue it is much more than that because it concludes with a number of kingdom moments. The story takes place in 2002, focusing on senior high school student Christine 'Lady Bird' McPherson and the fraught relationship she has with her mother. This is traced through a series of dramas that weave together school and family life. Christine's choice of the name Lady Bird is a particular site of conflict between mother and daughter. The high school has a Catholic foundation and the role of Christianity is a recurring element in the plot.

Eventually Lady Bird fulfils her dream and leaves school for college in New York, but remains unreconciled to her mother. It is here that what I call a series of kingdom moments occur. First, as she is unpacking in her room she discovers her father has slipped into her luggage some drafts of letters that her mother has written to her but not had the confidence to send. These are addressed to 'Christine' and acknowledge her love for her daughter and being sorry they have been at odds with each other. They also describe her twice as a 'miracle'. Lady Bird phones her father who says that he wants Lady Bird to know how her mother loves her.

Clearly affected by these letters, Lady Bird goes to a college party and begins a conversation with a stranger called David. This is the second kingdom moment. She asks him, 'Do you believe in God?'

He replies, 'Uh, no.'

She presses him, 'Why not?'

Clearly uncomfortable, he responds, 'Really? Uh, it's ridiculous!'

She reflects, 'People call each other by names their parents made up for them but they don't believe in God.' And she looks puzzled. She is then asked her name and says, 'Christine. My name's Christine.'

Christine proceeds to get very drunk and is carried from the party to hospital. When she wakes up she is next to a mother with a young son who has one eye covered with a bandage. When she leaves hospital Christine wanders into a church where a choir is singing. As she watches and listens to them, she appears to be close to tears. This is the third kingdom moment, and on leaving the church she phones home and leaves a message for her mother telling her how much she loves her.

There is nothing theologically heavy-handed about these kingdom moments, but there are elements of faith and religion at each point leading up to that instant of reconciliation. It could be argued that thoughts about miracles, questions about God and the emotional power of music are universal. That is all true, but such kingdom moments bring us back to a recurring theme in this chapter: kingdom stories give us glimpses of the kingdom of heaven – if we are open to seeing them.

7 Churches and kingdom stories

In *Leading by Story*, David Sims and I state:

> The church is a storytelling organization. It has a story to tell to those inside and outside, a story that it values and that it believes is worth telling. The Gospels frequently present Jesus as a storyteller, and many of the most loved passages of the Bible are stories. Storytelling is a sacred activity in the Christian faith. (Roberts and Sims, 2017, p. 39)

This chapter has begun to explore in greater detail the nature of stories in the Gospels and in Jesus' teaching, and how kingdom stories can reach out into the wider world beyond the Church.

Before moving on to Chapter 2 it would be helpful to address three questions: Why are kingdom stories important for the Church? Why are kingdom stories important for ministry? And why are kingdom stories important for leading and leaders?

The contention of this book is that kingdom stories are not confined to the Church. Yes, we see signs of God's kingdom inside the Body of Christ, and it is important for all those involved in leading churches to be attentive to those internal signals and stories. However, as we saw earlier in the work of Sam Wells, God's activity is not confined to the Church but is to be found abundantly in the wider world. One of the implications of this is whether it makes ecclesial and theological sense to have firm or rigid boundaries between the Church and the world. In his work on virtue ecclesiology, John Fitzmaurice puts it in this way:

> Perhaps two of the greatest challenges for the contemporary church are to understand if an identity of non-participation is ever appropriate, and how to engage (should it wish to) with those whose identity is based on an element of non-participation (Fitzmaurice, 2016, p. 107)

Or to put it another way, if God is active in stories beyond the Church and with those who are not participating in churches, how does the Body of Christ connect with those people, communities and their narratives? Being alert to kingdom stories is one of the ways in which the Church can fulfil that form of engagement. That is why they are important to churches and to ministry. Kingdom stories can be found in traditional manifestations of ministry such as baptisms, weddings and funerals. They can also be found in forms where churches seek to serve local communities through food banks, after-school clubs, projects to help those who are unemployed and more. But they can also be experienced in groups supporting those who are ex-offenders, who have experienced domestic abuse, who have additional or special needs, who face racism and discrimination, and many other contemporary personal and social challenges.

Finally, what about kingdom stories and leading? In his book on business leadership and narrative, Stephen Denning recounts this tale about what he calls the serendipitous development of sticky notes by 3M:

It took five years from the time Dr Spence Silver invented the peculiar substance – an adhesive that didn't stick very much – to the time a new-product development researcher named Art Fry came up with the Post-It note. Recalling his frustration at trying to keep his place in the church choir hymnal, Fry realized that Silver's 'failed' adhesive could make for a wonderfully reliable bookmark. (Denning, 2011, p. 142)

That is not a kingdom story in the sense that God's kingdom is revealed in and through an individual's or church's actions or behaviour. But it does illustrate how those involved in leading at whatever level can find sudden insight from unexpected places, such as the challenges of finding one's place in the church hymn book.

8 Kingdom stories: a preliminary summary

In this chapter we have examined the nature of 'kingdom' in Jesus' teaching and how it can be seen as a word that denotes God's action in our world. Furthermore, we have looked at how that kingdom or divine activity exists inside and outside the ministry of the Body of Christ and local churches. In the next chapter we shall take this a step further by exploring how specific stories about Jesus can interact with contemporary insights and concerns.

Jackson W. Carroll's helpful work on authority and leadership in ministry includes this observation about how the Gospel accounts of Jesus' life and current narratives interact:

> Jesus's story illumines, provides patterns for, and judges the story of God's people who came before and after those pivotal events, and it illumines and judges our own ongoing struggle to live faithfully within that narrative in the ever changing and complex circumstances in which we find ourselves. (Carroll, 2011, p. 74)

In terms of the ideas that David Sims and I set out in *Leading by Story* (2017), this chapter and the one that follows are exploring the Church's interpretive stories, in particular what we refer to as theological narratives (see Roberts and Sims, 2017, chapter 6). Within the context of ministry in local churches, having an understanding of the biblical and theological story in which those ministries are set is fundamental to leading those Christian and church communities. In Carroll's terms, it involves living and leading between Jesus' story and our stories.

With that in mind, in the next chapter we turn to a series of eight stories from the Gospels and bring them into conversation with ideas from organization studies and more expressions of artistic culture. I have deliberately chosen mainly non-biblical words as the headings for these reflections. This is to highlight both distance and proximity. The terms under consideration are: risk, followership, typologies, authenticity, purpose, meaning/wisdom, discipleship, trust. Some believe strongly that the study of organizations, management and leadership has little or nothing to do with the realities of life in first-century Palestine. While I would not want to downplay the historical and cultural differences between the two eras, like Carroll, I believe that illumination from one period to the other can be helpful for understanding the nature of ministry and stories of leadership.

Prayer

O God of vision and healing,
be with us as we seek your kingdom in our lives,
our communities and our imaginations;
may your Spirit grant us the wisdom to see your presence in
    our world
and your kingdom in our hearts;
we ask this in the name of Jesus, source of your incarnate love.
Amen.

On reflection

1 How do you understand Jesus' proclamation of God's kingdom?
2 Where do you discover or glimpse kingdom stories in your life and ministry?
3 What forms of art speak to you about the kingdom of God?

Notes

1 Helpful discussions can be found on different approaches to Jesus and eschatology in Witherington, 1995; Schwarz, 2000; Marsh and Moyise, 2015.

2 See sixth video from 6 minutes at www.alfiebradley.com/copy-of-introduction (accessed 23.4.19).

3 See www.coventrycathedral.org.uk/wpsite/blog/2019/02/16/knife-angel-coming-to-coventry/?doing_wp_cron=1556003303.3215789794 921875000000 (accessed 23.4.19).

4 https://en.wikipedia.org/wiki/Lady_Bird_(film) (accessed 16.4.19).

2

Jesus and Kingdom Stories

1 Introduction

In Chapter 1 we looked at the place of the kingdom in Jesus' proclamation of the good news and how we might see glimpses of God's ongoing activity and discover kingdom stories in today's world. We shall explore such an approach further in this chapter, specifically through eight kingdom stories from the life and ministry of Jesus. These are:

1 Jesus' temptations (Matthew 4.1–11).
2 The calling of the disciples (Mark 1.16–20).
3 The parable of the farmer and the seed (Luke 8.4–15).
4 Who do you say that I am (Mark 8.27–38)?
5 The cost of building a tower and going to war (Luke 14.25–33).
6 Let anyone with ears listen (Matthew 11.2–19).
7 Parable of the talents (Matthew 25.14–30).
8 Jesus washes the disciples' feet (John 13.2–16).

I shall continue to use art and popular culture as a means of highlighting God's presence in and through human experience but this chapter will extend this analysis by turning as well to another, often neglected, discipline – the study of organizations and leadership.

We have seen that a growing body of work on how organizations are storytelling and story-sharing communities (for example: Gabriel, 2000; Kostera, 2012; Mead, 2014; Roberts and Sims, 2017) can help to shed light on church ministry. In the same way that imaginative perceptions from art, poetry, films, music, novels and all forms of art can mediate God's kingdom, so can insights from organization studies. To this end, I shall be using learning from theories and practices of management to shape and inform an understanding of kingdom stories.

2 Kingdom stories and risk

Jesus' temptations (Matthew 4.1–11)

Then Jesus was led up by the Spirit into the wilderness to be tempted by the devil. He fasted for forty days and forty nights, and afterwards he was famished. The tempter came and said to him, 'If you are the Son of God, command these stones to become loaves of bread.' But he answered, 'It is written,

> "One does not live by bread alone,
> but by every word that comes from the mouth of God."'

Then the devil took him to the holy city and placed him on the pinnacle of the temple, saying to him, 'If you are the Son of God, throw yourself down; for it is written,

> "He will command his angels concerning you",
> and "On their hands they will bear you up,
> so that you will not dash your foot against a stone."'

Jesus said to him, 'Again it is written, "Do not put the Lord your God to the test."'

Again, the devil took him to a very high mountain and showed him all the kingdoms of the world and their splendour; and he said to him, 'All these I will give you, if you will fall down and worship me.' Jesus said to him, 'Away with you, Satan! for it is written,

> "Worship the Lord your God,
> and serve only him."'

Then the devil left him, and suddenly angels came and waited on him.

Journey and risk

Ministry is about risk and there is a great deal in Scripture about taking risks. Having said that, the word 'risk' (or a Hebrew/ Greek equivalent) does not appear in the Bible. So let's begin with a passage where risk is implied while not actually named. The story of Jesus' temptation in the wilderness is found in the Gospels of Matthew and Luke. It is well worth reading both accounts, and they are very similar, although Luke has the temptations in a different order. But I shall focus on Matthew's version, in part because he forges a stronger link between Jesus' baptism and his journey into the wilderness.

That intimate connection between God's calling and Jesus' immediate search for the true nature of his vocation is something that appeals to me. Jesus was called by God, but to what? As we hear in both accounts, the process of discerning the divine will was a difficult and demanding one. For Matthew's first hearers, those references to Jesus being in the wilderness for 40 days would have brought to mind the foundation story of Israel. This would have included Moses' encounter with God where he received the Torah: 'He was there with the LORD for forty days and forty nights; he neither ate bread nor drank water. And he wrote on the tablets the words of the covenant, the ten commandments' (Exodus 34.28).

The reference also creates a connection with the whole People of God being in the wilderness during their exodus from Egypt:

> Your children shall be shepherds in the wilderness for forty years, and shall suffer for your faithlessness, until the last of your dead bodies lies in the wilderness. According to the number of the days in which you spied out the land, forty days, for every day a year, you shall bear your iniquity, forty years, and you shall know my displeasure. (Numbers 14.33–34)

That specific period of time set apart also alludes to the prophetic ministry of Elijah: 'He got up, and ate and drank; then he went in the strength of that food for forty days and forty nights to Horeb the mount of God' (1 Kings 19.8).

Significantly, there are various other links in the Gospels between the accounts of Jesus and the story of Elijah – for example, at the transfiguration (Matthew 17.1–8; Mark 9.2–8; Luke 9.28–36) and his crucifixion (Matthew 11.2–19; Mark 15.36), and in Jesus' teaching immediately after the temptation story in Luke (Luke 4.15–26). At the heart of these references to 40 days and 40 nights is the idea that Jesus' own risky journey with God continues the walk started by Moses and the people of God, continued by Elijah and the prophets, and on into the time of the Messiah, God's Chosen One.

Journey and encounter

Those were journeys of great risk and much uncertainty but also journeys of encounter – receiving the Ten Commandments, being fed by the manna of God and hearing the voice of God not in the storm or earthquake but in the sound of sheer silence. We hear in the responses of both Moses and Elijah voices of uncertainty. Moses protests: 'Who am I that I should go to Pharaoh, and bring the Israelites out of Egypt?' (Exodus 3.11). And Elijah says not once but twice: 'I alone am left, and they are seeking my life, to take it away' (1 Kings 19.10, 14).

In my time as a director of ordinands and vocations adviser and helping people to explore their vocations, it has been an enormous privilege to hear people's stories of how they felt that God had called them in various different ways. Each of those stories was one of risk: 'Who am I that I should go ...?' Sometimes the journey can be a long one because of a tortuous route, or they have been resisting God's call. Other times it was sudden – God speaking unexpectedly out of Scripture, or someone making a suggestion such as, 'Have you ever thought about ministry in some form?'

In contemporary language, risk has been defined as: 'when we do not know in advance the outcomes of our actions. This is true in almost all situations, but the experience of risk becomes more challenging when those outcomes are not trivial' (Fineman, Sims and Gabriel, 2005, p. 391). The example given in their discussion is that of telling one's boss that they are wrong. Exploring a call from God is never trivial and we certainly do not know in advance the outcomes of our actions. That was most certainly the case for Moses, Elijah, Jesus and their kingdom stories.

Journey and call

Listening to other individuals' stories of their call from God does not necessarily make it any less risky when it comes to one's own vocation. For me, one call from God came while sitting in Bath Abbey waiting for a concert by the Tallis Scholars and getting a strong sense of God calling me to a new stage of ministry. That sense of calling deepened during the concert and in the days ahead.

That was the start of a journey that led to Warwick. I was not placed on one of the abbey's pinnacles and given a vision. It was more like John Wesley's experience of his heart being 'strangely warmed'. The signposts were not immediately clear, and even when I had been offered and accepted the post of team rector there were still moments when I had to stand with Elijah before the silence of God and listen intently for what the divine whisper was saying. Part of the reason for that is because our stories are not written independently of others. If we have a spouse, how does a new chapter in my story affect his or her story? If we have children, the same question applies. Are we caring for parents or other dependants? What about those friendships we value – we may be supporting them, they may be supporting us? All of that changes the moment we embrace risk and respond to God's call.

And that does not just apply to those moments of significant change in our personal vocation. Risk is present too when we feel called to make changes in the life of those churches that

JESUS AND KINGDOM STORIES

we are serving. Is it time to start a new form of worship? Is it right to bring something to an end and say that its season has now passed? Is this unexpected development a prompt from God or is it a marker along the way, that in God's time we will need to come back to this cairn to build, act or take another risk? Within the context of a church, that process of discerning God's action in our world and our lives, sharing and speaking about that to others and leading the kingdom story is the dynamic with which this book is concerned.

Vocation and risk

Jesus' journey into the wilderness tested and refined his calling from God. It was the start of his ongoing pilgrimage of risk that eventually led to the ultimate sacrifice on the cross of Calvary. On that road and later in Matthew's Gospel, Jesus says to his disciples: 'Truly I tell you, unless you change and become like children, you will never enter the kingdom of heaven' (Matthew 18.3).

Theologians and scholars have reflected deeply about what that image and those words imply. Let me add a further suggestion. In their book *The Trusted Leader* (2002), Robert Galford and Anne Seibold Drapeau observe:

> The way kids learn is by taking risks. The only way they take risks is if they feel safe enough to extend themselves. And if they do it once, and don't get burned, they'll do it again, and again. That's how they grow. (p. 127)

In our life, our vocation, our ministry there will undoubtedly be times when we are called to follow Christ into the wilderness and to take risks. Those risks will be great and small and we will need to learn to become like children and enter the kingdom of risk.

Kingdom stories and risk

For those involved in the ministry of Christ's body in all its many forms, it is important to see that risk is a vital element. Whenever Christians speak out about God's kingdom in the public domain they take a risk. In a 'Thought for the Day' on Radio 4's *Today* programme in 1984, Bishop Jim Thompson reflected on how a leading politician had suggested that clergy should give up politics for Lent. The Bishop observed that Lent is a time when the Church focuses on Jesus' 40 days in the wilderness and his time of prayer about his role. Thompson went on:

> The difficulty about giving up political issues for Lent – which would itself be a relief – is that we would have to give up praying as well. Concern about the special social-political issues of our day grows out of prayer. Involvement is what counts to people and lends urgency to our need to pray. (Thompson, 1991, p. 88)

A generation later it is still perfectly possible for issues such as food banks or an archbishop speaking at a TUC conference to generate controversy. When Archbishop Justin Welby spoke to the TUC in 2018, he tweeted that morning: 'I'm often told that Archbishops should "stick to religious and spiritual matters" and "stay out of politics". I have a feeling today might be another one of those days.' Kingdom stories inevitably involve risk. We can see that in the accounts of Jesus' temptations – and even before that. Mary's yes to God at the annunciation (Luke 1.26–38), the journey of Mary and Joseph to Bethlehem (Luke 2.1–7) and the holy family's flight to Egypt (Matthew 2.13–23) were all very risky undertakings.

They may not always be of the same magnitude, but listening to and engaging with the kingdom stories of our communities and bringing their concerns to God in prayer, caring for those who are in need and speaking out on issues of the day are just some of the ways that the Church can take risks on behalf of

God's kingdom, incarnate Christ's presence in our world and nurture the fruits of the Spirit in our lives.

Prayer

O God of risk,
you entered our world to proclaim
the good news of your kingdom revealed in Christ;
bless us and all who take risks for you,
be with us in times of testing
and be our guide as we respond to your calling in our lives;
for your name's sake. Amen.

On reflection

1 When and where have you taken risks and what were the outcomes?
2 What have you learnt from this about risk-taking for God's kingdom?
3 Where do you see God leading you to take risks in the future?

3 Kingdom stories and followership

The calling of the disciples (Mark 1.16–20)

> As Jesus passed along the Sea of Galilee, he saw Simon and his brother Andrew casting a net into the lake – for they were fishermen. And Jesus said to them, 'Follow me and I will make you fish for people.' And immediately they left their nets and followed him. As he went a little farther, he saw James son of Zebedee and his brother John, who were in their boat mending the nets. Immediately he called them; and they left their father Zebedee in the boat with the hired men, and followed him.

How do we follow?

Take a bit of time to think about your faith journey. Was there a moment when you became a follower of Christ? Some can point to a precise instant at which they started to follow in Jesus' way. Having attended numerous Christian Union meetings as a student and as a university chaplain, I have been present at many calls for people to make a decision for Christ. However, for others their path has been smoother or more consistent. They may have been taken to church as a child or been to a school where assemblies or chapel were part of everyday life.

While training for ministry, a group of us went to see and hear Billy Graham at a sports stadium, and were very shocked when one of our number went forward after the famous evangelist issued his call for people to come out and commit their lives to Christ. We quizzed him afterwards and he clearly did not see his action as a moment of conversion but something more akin to a renewal of baptismal vows and part of his ongoing journey. For some, faith is a steady progression; for others it is an instant of conversion. For some it can be a combination of the two, and for yet others it can be something else entirely.

The Australian poet Peter Kocan has a lovely verse entitled 'Cathedral Service', which describes an accidental encounter with Christian faith during a service of choral evensong that he wandered into.

I'm only here because I wandered in
Not knowing that a service would begin,
And had to slide into the nearest pew,
Pretending it was what I'd meant to do.

The tall candles cast their frail light
Upon the priest, the choir clad in white,
The carved and polished and embroidered scene,
The congregation numbers seventeen.

And awkwardly I follow as I'm led
To kneel or stand or sing or bow my head.
Though these specific rites are strange to me,
I know their larger meaning perfectly –

The heritage of twenty centuries
Is symbolised in rituals like these,
In special modes of beauty and of grace
Enacted in a certain kind of place.

This faith, although I lack it, is my own,
Inherent to the marrow of the bone.
To this even the unbelieving mind
Submits its unbelief to be defined.

Perhaps the meagre congregation shows
How all of that is drawing to a close,
And remnants only come here to entreat
These dying flickers of the obsolete.

Yet when did this religion ever rest
On weight of numbers as the final test?
Its founder said that it was all the same
When two or three were gathered in his name.[1]

There is nothing in this encounter that speaks of heavenly glory or the power of God. This is an intimate yet also hesitant encounter with the divine, which is movingly described across the fourth and fifth stanzas in these lines:

> In special modes of beauty and of grace
> Enacted in a certain kind of place.
> This faith, although I lack it, is my own,
> Inherent to the marrow of the bone.

On the one hand, Kocan acknowledges this faith that he lacks, while on the other it is part of the very marrow of his bone. We do not know what his personal story is from these verses but this poem describes how many in Western society feel about Christianity – it remains part of people's wider cultural life but not something to which they can commit for whatever reason. The journey over that threshold into being a follower of Christ takes many forms.

Being a follower

Although people's experience of becoming or not becoming a follower of Jesus is replete with many varied stories, the nature of *being* a follower is less well appreciated. For instance, being a follower has not been as widely studied as being a leader, although that is beginning to change. There is a growing field of political, business and academic analysis of what leadership involves with varying degrees of quality, but the study of followership, or what it means to be a follower, lags well behind. Barbara Kellerman (2008) has identified five different forms of follower, which she calls the Isolate, Bystander, Participant, Activist, Diehard. So being a follower is not to be part of a uniform or monochrome culture.

Briefly, Kellerman describes Isolates as being completely detached and not caring about their leaders. The example she discusses is drawn from politics and includes those who say that they are not interested in the political process, leaving their leaders to make decisions on their behalf. This is the most detached form of followership. Bystanders observe but do not participate. They stand aside from the group dynamics. In effect, Kellerman argues, this is tacit support for whatever constitutes the status quo. Participants are in some way engaged and have views about the leaders of those organizations in which they invest time, money and energy. Activists are eager, energetic and engaged because they feel strongly about their leaders. They will work tirelessly on their behalf, but equally can work hard to remove them if they fall short of expectation. Finally, Diehards are willing to give everything on behalf of a leader, an idea or both. Kellerman says that 'Being a Diehard is all-consuming. It is who you are. It determines what you do' (Kellerman, 2008, p. 92).

Jesus' followers

Jesus has an interesting approach to followers. We know he had different groups of followers and we can map some of those on to Kellerman's model. It is difficult to find an example of an Isolate in the Gospels because they are essentially a record of those who positively engaged with or firmly rejected Jesus' vision of God's kingdom. There were undoubtedly those who were not at all interested in the religious and social disputes of their time but they do not make their way into the New Testament.

There were certainly multitudes of Bystanders who came to hear Jesus preach and see him heal, such as the crowds at the feeding of the five thousand or at the Sermon on the Mount. For example, Mark sets the scene for the first miraculous feeding by saying how Jesus and the disciples went away in the boat to a deserted place by themselves:

Now many saw them going and recognized them, and they hurried there on foot from all the towns and arrived ahead of them. As he went ashore, he saw a great crowd; and he had compassion for them, because they were like sheep without a shepherd; and he began to teach them many things. (Mark 6.33–34)

There were curious Participants, such as Zacchaeus, the tax collector at Jericho who climbed a tree to see Jesus (Luke 19.1–10), and the rich young man who came to him asking about eternal life: 'Jesus, looking at him, loved him and said, "You lack one thing: go, sell what you own, and give the money to the poor, and you will have treasure in heaven; they come, follow me"' (Mark 10.21). And we can also see examples of Activists, such as the wider group that Jesus sent out to share his proclamation: 'The Lord appointed seventy others and sent them on ahead of him in pairs to every town and place where he himself intended to go. He said to them, "The harvest is plentiful, but the labourers are few"' (Luke 10.1–2).

And then there were the Diehards, such as the 12 disciples: '[Jesus] went up the mountain and called to him those whom he wanted, and they came to him. And he appointed twelve, whom he also named apostles, to be with him, and to be sent out to proclaim the message' (Mark 3.13–14). We can even identify an inner group of Diehards in the intimate core of disciples (Peter, James and John) that Jesus took aside with him at various times and who witnessed the transfiguration (Matthew 17.1–8; Mark 9.2–8; Luke 9.28–36).

However, the most significant point here is not that we can map Jesus' followers neatly on to Kellerman's approach. A key element is that followers come in diverse forms. We can see it in the Gospels and we can see it too in contemporary churches and communities. It is important to note that, by and large, Jesus does not stand in judgement on those who come to hear him. He expresses sorrow that the rich young man is not able to follow him and some exasperation when two of his own Diehards want to sit in the places of highest honour on his left and right (Matthew 20.20–28). He is frustrated with those from the Sadducees, Pharisees, Scribes who use their scriptural and religious authority to condemn their co-religionists (Matthew 12.1–7; John 8.1–11). Jesus proclaims God's kingdom in words and stories and allows his hearers to make their own responses. So how do we respond in our own time?

Kingdom stories and following

The Episcopalian priest Bill Countryman observes that for most people the first objective of being called is to pay attention to the life in which we find ourselves. We see something of this in those occasions when Jesus encounters people but does not encourage them to join his group. As Luke recounts:

> The man from whom the demons had gone begged that he might be with him; but Jesus sent him away, saying, 'Return to your home, and declare how much God has done for you.' So he went away, proclaiming throughout the city how much Jesus had done for him. (Luke 8.38–39; see also Mark 5.18–19)

Kingdom stories can always be found wherever we are. Countryman acknowledges this when he says that our calling to follow

> may indeed take us away from our familiar environment and lead us on a pilgrimage to new places or new kinds of life where we practice our priesthood. It may lead to a new sort of work, to a community hitherto strange to us, or to service to neighbors whose very existence meant nothing to us before. Yet, for most of us, most of the time, our priesthood simply calls us deeper within our present life, not away from it. (Countryman, 1999, p. 177)

The theologian Ann Morisy puts it in these terms: 'There is an invitation at the heart of every story that is shared. It is the invitation "You come too"' (Morisy, 2004, p. 114). Not only do followers themselves take different forms but the way in which people are called to follow in Christ's way varies too. Some are called to explore and find kingdom stories on a journey to the unfamiliar and the new, while others are called to stay and discover them in that which is known and recognized. And yet others find that going on some kind of spiritual or physical pilgrimage is the only way that they can discover how it is they are called to follow and where it is they are meant to find their kingdom stories. For me, something of this is captured in this old folk tale:

There was a man who grew tired of corruption in the world. His friends would listen as he spoke passionately of his desire for a city where God's justice was honoured and God's peace reigned. Night after night he would dream of a land free from discord and a city where heaven touched earth.

Then one day he announced he could wait no longer. He packed some food, said goodbye to his friends and set off to search for the city of his dreams. He walked all day and just before sunset he found a place to sleep just off the road, in a forest. He ate his sandwiches, said his prayers and smoothed down the ground for his bed. Just before he went to sleep, he placed his shoes in the centre of the path, pointing in the direction that he would continue the next day.

As he slept, a stranger walking the same path discovered the traveller's shoes. Unable to resist a joke, the stranger turned the shoes around so they pointed in the direction from which the traveller had come.

Early next morning the traveller arose, said his prayers, ate what remained of his food and started his journey, walking in the direction that his shoes pointed. He walked all day long and just before the sun set he could see a city in the distance. Was this the city of his dreams? It certainly looked familiar. As he entered the city, he seemed to recognise the streets. As he walked he recognised the houses; and when he came to what he recognised as his own house he knew that the heavenly city where he was meant to find peace and justice was indeed his own city that he had set off from. (White, 1986, p. 92)

This story relates directly to Francis Thompson's poem 'The Kingdom of God' and to an engaged eschatology discussed earlier. In the same way that Thompson identifies Jacob's ladder at Charing Cross, and Genesareth alongside the River Thames, this story identifies the heavenly city as the traveller's home. Being a follower of Jesus may involve a physical journey to discover signs of God's kingdom in unfamiliar places but it can equally require a spiritual journey to find the kingdom of heaven within ourselves, and yet again it may require an engagement with both types of pilgrimage. We shall discuss followership further in the next chapter, when we consider the Church and kingdom stories.

Prayer

O Christ,
you have called us to follow in your way
and are present with us on all our journeys;
strengthen us for all that lies ahead
and guide our feet as we seek your kingdom;
wherever you lead, may we be held in your grace;
we ask this in the name of the One who is the way, the truth
    and the life. Amen.

On reflection

1 What is the story of your becoming a follower of Christ?
2 Do you recognize different forms of follower in the churches in which you have been involved?
3 How can we develop the way we invite people into our kingdom stories?

Note

1 Peter Kocan, *Standing with Friends*, Port Melbourne: Heinemann, 1992, p. 44. 'Cathedral Service' and other poems by Peter Kocan can be found online at www.andrewlansdown.com/other-poets-poems/peter-kocan/.

4 Kingdom stories and typologies

Parable of the farmer and the seed (Luke 8.4–15)

> When a great crowd gathered and people from town after town came to [Jesus], he said in a parable: 'A sower went out to sow his seed; and as he sowed, some fell on the path and was trampled on, and the birds of the air ate it up. Some fell on the rock; and as it grew up, it withered for lack of moisture. Some fell among thorns, and the thorns grew with it and choked it. Some fell into good soil, and when it grew, it produced a hundredfold.' As he said this, he called out, 'Let anyone with ears to hear listen!'
>
> Then his disciples asked him what this parable meant. He said, 'To you it has been given to know the secrets of the kingdom of God; but to others I speak in parables, so that
>
> "looking they may not perceive,
>> and listening they may not understand."
>
> 'Now the parable is this: The seed is the word of God. The ones on the path are those who have heard; then the devil comes and takes away the word from their hearts, so that they may not believe and be saved. The ones on the rock are those who, when they hear the word, receive it with joy. But these have no root; they believe only for a while and in a time of testing fall away. As for what fell among the thorns, these are the ones who hear; but as they go on their way, they are choked by the cares and riches and pleasures of life, and their fruit does not mature. But as for that in the good soil, these are the ones who, when they hear the word, hold it fast in an honest and good heart, and bear fruit with patient endurance.'

The parable of the farmer and the seed has a number of challenges in terms of theology and interpretation. For instance, some commentators have suggested that the parable's explanation owes more to the early Church than to Jesus.[1] Furthermore, was Jesus' use of parables meant to hide his message, or is this an after-the-fact explanation by his followers? More specifically, did *both* disciples and bystanders often miss the point of his illustrations at the time, and is this passage (at least in part) an explanation from the early Church as to why this happened?

My aim here is not to resolve such contested issues of interpretation, important though they are, but to present the parable as a primary example of the Christian faith using a simple typology or model of the different listeners who were receiving Jesus' message. The way in which the parable is presented in Luke and the other Synoptic Gospels sets out four types of hearer and their responses to Jesus' words. It is one answer to the more complex question: why did people not respond to Jesus' proclamation about God's kingdom? Or, to put it another way: how come all this happened?

Human organizations are by nature complicated and involved. Churches are complex too and it is no accident that the term 'byzantine' is used to describe over-elaborate organizations. That is one of the reasons why typologies are so appealing. They reduce this organizational complexity into a manageable form. Typology is not a word that is widely used or discussed in either church or leadership circles. It does not generate a great deal of excitement. Other terms are more frequently used, such as models, metaphors or images, but they are, in essence, typologies. Daniel Katz and Robert L. Kahn provide this helpful summary after describing a breadth of social types: 'The many organizational models illustrate the differing systems in which social theorists have been interested, and the difficulty of bringing a very complex set of phenomena into a single framework' (Katz and Kahn, 1978, p. 285). In other words, typologies and models enable us to manage organizational complexity.

I have used typologies in my own work, most recently Yiannis Gabriel's 'ecology of story' (Gabriel, 2016) in *Leading by Story* (Roberts and Sims, 2017).[2] However, my first introduction to typologies for Christianity and for churches came when I studied for a year in Chicago at McCormick Theological Seminary. One of the courses preparing students for Presbyterian ministry in the USA was entitled 'Contexts of Ministry',[3] which involved visiting a wide range of congregations and faith communities across the city – from the predominantly white and cathedral-like Fourth Presbyterian Church to a predominantly black Pentecostal church, from Willow Creek to a Unification Church (better known as the 'Moonies'). That breadth of ecclesial experience has been an important element in shaping my approach to ministry.

The reading for this course involved Avery Dulles' *Models of the Church* (1978) and H. Richard Niebuhr's *Christ and Culture* (1951), both of which involved typologies. Dulles identifies five different forms of church from his perspective as a Catholic theologian:

Avery Dulles' models of the church

- Church as Institution – an ordered, structured and stable society.
- Church as Mystical Communion – a relational community representing the Body of Christ.
- Church as Sacrament – a symbolic expression of God's grace in Christ.
- Church as Herald – a community for proclaiming the gospel.
- Church as Servant – seeking to live out the kingdom in serving the world.

Niebuhr classified five different approaches that churches take to their surrounding culture from his standpoint as a Protestant theologian:

H. Richard Niebuhr's taxonomy of Christ and culture

- Christ against Culture – Christianity's opposition to culture.
- The Christ of Culture – accommodation between Christianity and culture.
- Christ above Culture – Christ as the fulfilment of culture.
- Christ and Culture in Paradox – ongoing tension between Christ and culture.
- Christ the Transformer of Culture – Jesus as the converter of culture and society.

These two typologies have been extensively critiqued since their publication but their appeal and the attraction of many other ways of modelling human behaviour have continued in practical theology and organizational studies. For example, Bill Hybels' (2002) typology of ten approaches to leadership (visionary, directional, strategic, managing, motivational, shepherding, team-building entrepreneurial, re-engineering, bridge-building) has been clearly influential in, say, Lamdin's *Finding Your Leadership Style* (2012).[4]

We can see the attraction of typologies in organization theory as well. We have already discussed Barbara Kellerman's classification of followers (Chapter 2.3). There are further examples in Gareth Morgan's *Images of Organization* (1997) and Monika Kostera's *Organizations and Archetypes* (2012), while Mintzberg, Ahlstrand and Lampel (1998) have provided an extensive categorization of different approaches to strategy, and, returning to leadership, Alvesson and Spicer's *Metaphors We Lead By* (2011) is a thoroughly secular approach that nevertheless concludes by drawing attention to the 'almost *sacred* character' of leadership (p. 197 – emphasis added), which we will consider further in Chapter 3. In some church circles, Don Clifton's strengthfinder typology is used for leadership training and it is arguable that the Natural Church Development (NCD) programme outlining the eight characteristics for healthy churches is also a form of typology (Roberts and Sims, 2017, pp. 150–79). But how do all these different typologies work out in practice, and how do they relate to our kingdom stories?

Kingdom stories and typology

We began with a typology from the Gospels – Jesus' parable about the farmer sowing seed in a field and how the different results can be used to illustrate the different responses to his message. In its most succinct form the parable answers the question, 'How come?' How come many of Jesus' listeners missed his message? It could be argued that all typologies answer the question, 'How come?' How come churches have different forms? How come the various churches take different approaches to their surrounding cultures? How come there are different forms of leadership and followership, strategy and organizational understanding?

In the time since studying in Chicago and visiting many different expressions of church life, I have kept in touch with two friends who were also on the 'Contexts of Ministry' course. We have continued to discuss what we learnt then and how it has (or hasn't) applied to our ministries – one with the Church of England and two with the Presbyterian Church in the USA. In my view, there are two key lessons.

First, as already mentioned, the typologies of Dulles and Niebuhr continue to have resonance even now. In 2015 I spent some time with a group undertaking an MA in church leadership and shared with them some of the ideas being worked on for *Leading by Story* (2017). Dulles' ideas were still being taught and shared as part of that masters course, while John Fitzmaurice has revisited Niebuhr's work in his *Virtue Ecclesiology* (2016, pp. 59–61). Thus, both Dulles and Niebuhr's work continue to be part of the 'How come?' conversations around the Church, and although it is possible to map churches on to these typologies, that is not the key element in my view. More importantly, a taxonomy of metaphors or images helps us work with the inevitable organizational diversity in churches. As Katz and Kahn point out, such approaches help those coping with organizational complexity to bring a sense of order to their situation or context (1978, pp. 259–92).

Second, if we want to answer the 'How come?' questions about a church, then *context* is fundamental. When the Church is engaged in ministry in a specific place, the starting point is to ask, 'What are the stories that speak of God's kingdom in this situation, whether that's a town, village, hospital, school or wherever we find ourselves in ministry?' And we should not forget that when we are exploring how the body of Christ continues to be incarnate in a particular setting, the metaphor of the body is itself an image of diversity.[5]

Every congregation will certainly include different models of the Church, various ways to relate to the surrounding culture, and different understandings of leadership. This is part of the organizational complexity of Christianity that goes back not only to the early Church but to the first disciples called by Jesus. And we can see the Church using forms of typology to address that from the beginning. Indeed, the parable of the sower shows Jesus using a typology that would be easily understood by his audience to illustrate part of the kingdom story that he was proclaiming. The ways in which people responded to Jesus' kingdom story were many and various, and that remains true in our own time. We shall examine this narrative diversity further in the detailed analysis of one particular kingdom story in Chapter 4.

Prayer

O God of all creation,
you scatter the seed of your grace and love;
help us to tend your seedlings with care,
and nurture all your plants, that they may flourish;
so your kingdom may blossom in the world and the Church;
through Jesus Christ our saviour. Amen.

On reflection

1 Are there other typologies that you have found helpful in thinking about ministry?
2 What 'How come?' conversations are you having at the moment?
3 Has your context of ministry changed or is it changing now? What have you learnt from changing contexts?

Notes

1 'It is usually accepted that the interpretation of the parable of the sower that follows (vv. 11–15) owes more to the early church than Jesus himself' (Franklin, 2001, p. 937).

2 I have discussed typologies further in Roberts, 2008, and Roberts, 2017b, pp. 10–12.

3 Surprisingly, the word 'context' may have been a neologism introduced into common usage by Thomas Cranmer in the sixteenth century (MacCulloch, 2018, p. 189).

4 Hybels was founding pastor of Willow Creek Church. In 2018 he resigned as senior pastor following accusations of sexual misconduct, charges he continues to deny. Nevertheless, the pros and cons of his leadership principles continue to be debated and it is significant that the worldwide Willow Creek network of churches has been rebranded the 'Global Leadership Network'.

5 For a detailed analysis of how the body works as a metaphor for churches, see Roberts, 2000.

5 Kingdom stories and authenticity

Who do you say that I am? (Mark 8.27–38)

> Jesus went on with his disciples to the villages of Caesarea
> Philippi; and on the way he asked his disciples, 'Who do people
> say that I am?' And they answered him, 'John the Baptist; and
> others, Elijah; and still others, one of the prophets.' He asked
> them, 'But who do you say that I am?' Peter answered him, 'You
> are the Messiah.' And he sternly ordered them not to tell anyone
> about him.
>
> Then he began to teach them that the Son of Man must undergo
> great suffering, and be rejected by the elders, the chief priests,
> and the scribes, and be killed, and after three days rise again. He
> said all this quite openly. And Peter took him aside and began to
> rebuke him. But turning and looking at his disciples, he rebuked
> Peter and said, 'Get behind me, Satan! For you are setting your
> mind not on divine things but on human things.'
>
> He called the crowd with his disciples, and said to them, 'If any
> want to become my followers, let them deny themselves and take
> up their cross and follow me. For those who want to save their life
> will lose it, and those who lose their life for my sake, and for the
> sake of the gospel, will save it. For what will it profit them to gain
> the whole world and forfeit their life? Indeed, what can they give
> in return for their life? Those who are ashamed of me and of my
> words in this adulterous and sinful generation, of them the Son
> of Man will also be ashamed when he comes in the glory of his
> Father with the holy angels.'

There is a sense in which Jesus' question to his disciples, 'Who
do people say that I am?' and Peter's response, 'You are the
Messiah', is the point at which Mark's Gospel turns. Not only
is this a clear moment of insight into Jesus' identity, but there
is also a sharp distinction between 'divine things' and 'human
things'. In Mark's account, this is the first of three passion

predictions, and the serious nature of the language – speaking about God's things and rebuking one another – indicates that this story takes us deep into the heart of the mystery of the kingdom (Perrin, 2018, pp. 255–7).

Jesus is revealing his fullest self-understanding with the disciples, plus his understanding of God's kingdom, some of which he goes on to share with the crowd that is following them. We have a profound sense that we are hearing the authentic Jesus telling us his story and what it truly means. And not only is Jesus showing who he is, he is also giving an unambiguous indication of where his story is going, and that is what Peter finds so disconcerting.

Authenticity has become an important part of contemporary culture. In her 2018 TED Talk, Herminia Ibarra, a professor of organizational behaviour, begins by saying that in her view we have reached 'peak authenticity'. The quantity of work published, spoken and discussed on this subject has reached its high point.[1]

So what is authenticity and how do we recognize authentic leadership? In their analysis of authentic leadership, Rob Goffee and Gareth Jones identify three characteristics for authentic leaders (Goffee and Jones, 2006, p. 16):

1 Consistency between words and deeds – they 'practise what they preach'.
2 Coherence in different roles – they communicate consistently with different audiences.
3 Comfort with self – they have an inner core that coheres with how they perform.

A crucial element in this is being genuine or sincere – saying what you mean and meaning what you say. Ibarra notes that the origins of the word 'sincere' lie in the Roman world, where it meant 'without wax' (*sine cera*). It was common practice for those making and selling statues to hide any flaws in their statues by using wax. Those merchants who were more scrupulous in their business practices would put up a sign saying 'sine cera', in order that customers would know the authentic nature of their products.

The problem with this analogy is that if sincere means 'without wax' then it implies that authentic leadership is flawless, and we know from all kinds of experience that few (if any) of those who are leading can match such a high standard. And furthermore, no church or organization is ever flawless either. By contrast, genuine authenticity must not only be aware of whatever flaws we have but also possess insight into what the implications of those weaknesses might be. And this is for two reasons.

First, an understanding of our shortcomings is vital to that consistency between words and deeds that I have just mentioned. If we do not have an astute perception of these then it is highly likely we will not end up practising what we preach. And we could also be found wanting on the third characteristic of authentic leadership, being comfortable with oneself.

Second, if people who are leading do not know their flaws then it will have a significantly negative impact on whatever organization they are leading. No individual is the complete leader in the sense of having all the skills and gifts that a church or community requires. And it is only by knowing which of these abilities they lack that leaders can look out for those with whom they need to share the responsibilities of leadership. Therefore, authenticity and sincerity (in the modern sense) are important for leading, but so is a clear-sighted perspective of our flaws.

Ibarra is aware of this need for self-understanding up to a point, because she describes it in what she calls the 'authenticity paradox'. This is a situation in which people get caught between doing what it takes to be effective and their values or integrity. The example she gives is when she knew her teaching was not good enough and she had to change her approach to one that did not come naturally to her. She argues that we cannot think our way out of this paradox but rather we have to act our way out, while remaining true to our values.

This can certainly be true. Not everyone who preaches well necessarily begins like that. The same can be true of every aspect of ministry, from administration to youth work. Some skills have to be learnt and some roles inhabited before they become natural. Ibarra remarks that authenticity comes from the Greek, meaning 'that which you do with your own hands', and can mean the outcome of a creative process in which you are self-authoring. However, authenticity in leading and leadership go beyond individuals and their particular stories. Our own stories are undoubtedly significant, but we have to go further. Goffee and Jones point us in that direction when they say:

> Our observations have led us to the view that an authentic sense of self arises from individuals coming to terms with their own biography – and a critical part of this is to understand how their origins have come to shape them. Origins, of course, can be conceived of in many ways. For some family origin is most salient; for others it may be class, gender, ethnicity, social status, religion, or geographical locale. (Goffee and Jones, 2006, p. 52)

In other words, our own stories are part of a much wider collection of narratives, which we have to understand and integrate.

Whether we are leading, following or (most likely) doing both, we will be weaving our stories into those of other people, churches, communities, organizations, cultural narratives and more (Roberts and Sims, 2017). The challenge that everyone faces is how we can undertake this complex process in a way that is creative, authentic and true to everyone who is involved. This is where we come back to Jesus' discussion with his disciples at Caesarea Philippi and especially his question, 'Who do you say that I am?'

Kingdom stories and authenticity

As we reflect on this it is worth noting that while 'authenticity' and 'author' have different roots, they have grown very close

KINGDOM STORIES

in today's world. In churches and any organization, a very high
premium is placed on those people who can write (author) stories that are genuine (authentic). How do we set about writing
stories that are perceived as authentic? Ibarra would say that
it requires those who are leading to work through the authenticity paradox of being effective yet true to one's values. In
theological terms, I would say this is about vocation.

We know from Scripture and the experience of those around
us that everyone's vocation is different. We may be called
through a sense of longing or through our gifts, a sudden
voice from God or steady prompting over a period of time.
More often than not, like Jacob at the ford of Jabbok (Genesis
32.22–32), we have to wrestle with the angel of God's calling to us. In this process people change. Jacob becomes Israel,
Jabbok becomes Peniel, and those around us can be changed
too. This is a further example of Thompson's poetic insight
from our previous chapter about how the ladder to heaven can
extend from wherever we are.

But in addition, we can see this too with Jesus' wrestling
with Peter and his disciples at Caesarea Philippi and at other
points on his journey. Jesus is seeking and seeing his calling
from God, but even those close to him fundamentally disagree:
Peter took him aside and began to rebuke him. Jesus knows
where his story must go and how his story rewrites the expected
narrative of Jerusalem and God's people. Taking Goffee and
Jones' three characteristics of authentic leadership – consistency, coherence and comfort (with oneself) – we can identify
those throughout Jesus' life and through to his death.

Significantly, Goffee and Jones go on to argue that:

In order to properly engage others, leaders need to construct
a compelling narrative. They must find ways of looking at the
world that allows others not only to understand their role in
it but also to be excited by it. This does not mean rejecting
reasonable analysis. Rather, effective leaders bring their case
alive through rich examples, personal experiences, analogies,
and stories. (Goffee and Jones, 2006, p. 164)

At Caesarea Philippi, Jesus is sharing his compelling personal narrative, his deepest understanding of God's kingdom story, and it is being rejected by his followers. In the words of Richard Rohr about this passage, 'Too many people join a club instead of going on a journey toward God, love, or truth' (1997, p. 87). Authenticity is about being willing to embrace and tell the kingdom story of our journeys, rather than seeking out the security of the club, group or even the Church.

Prayer

Creator God, we are made in your image
and you call us to follow in the way of Christ;
be with us on our journeys wherever you may lead,
sustain us in that calling, that we may recognize signs of
  your kingdom
and consistently proclaim the story of your good news;
through him who is your incarnate Word. Amen.

On reflection

1 How are you able to maintain authenticity and be true to your God-given self?
2 What abilities do you lack in ministry and leadership?
3 Who in your team can provide those other, necessary gifts?

Note

1 Her talk is available at: www.youtube.com/watch?v=CIjI3TmEzrs (accessed 30.9.19).

6 Kingdom stories and purpose

The cost of building a tower and going to war (Luke 14.25–33)

> Large crowds were travelling with [Jesus], and he turned and said to them, 'Whoever comes to me and does not hate father and mother, wife and children, brothers and sisters, yes, and even life itself, cannot be my disciple. Whoever does not carry the cross and follow me cannot be my disciple. For which of you, intending to build a tower, does not first sit down and estimate the cost, to see whether he has enough to complete it? Otherwise, when he has laid a foundation and is not able to finish, all who see it will begin to ridicule him, saying, "This fellow began to build and was not able to finish." Or what king, going out to wage war against another king, will not sit down first and consider whether he is able with ten thousand to oppose the one who comes against him with twenty thousand? If he cannot, then, while the other is still far away, he sends a delegation and asks for the terms of peace. So therefore, none of you can become my disciple if you do not give up all your possessions.'

On the face of it, Jesus' parable about someone planning to build a tower and a king preparing for a war seems to be about two individuals and their purposes. However, as N. T. Wright argues, the reference to 'possessions' here is significant: 'Family and property, then, were not for the ancient Jew simply what they are to the modern western world. Both carried religious and cultural significance far beyond personal, let alone "individual", identity and security' (Wright, 1996, p. 405). Therefore, Jesus' examples of individuals bringing their purposes and plans to fruition have important social elements to them and are placed within a shared setting of discipleship and religious faith.

Ruth Etchells sees these parables in everyday terms. Jesus

could be speaking about a farmer who wishes to impress the neighbours or commenting about the land he was walking through, which would have been pock-marked by signs of war (Etchells, 1998, p. 129). By contrast, Nicholas Perrin has suggested that the builder of the tower and the king going to war are both Jesus himself (Perrin, 2018, pp. 120–2). The most grandiose building project of that time was Herod's stop-start Temple in Jerusalem. In Perrin's reading, the 'tower' is a reference to the 'temple', and the lack of planning is a critique of the Herodian family line, which is common in Luke's Gospel. It could also anticipate Luke 20.9–18, where Jesus is presented as both the true cornerstone and the true builder of the temple.

Earlier in Luke's narrative, Jesus is described as addressing a 'crowd gathered in thousands' (Luke 12.1), and Perrin reads the reference to a king planning a war against another ruler in terms of Gideon, who dramatically reduced his army by thousands upon God's instruction (Judges 7.2–23). Thus, for Perrin:

> Jesus wants to ensure that his own numerical strength not be mistaken as the means by which divine victory would be achieved. To achieve this ideal size, Jesus would reduce his army, much like Gideon, by screening out those of fragile resolve. (Perrin, 2018, p. 121)

To read Jesus' parable in this way also places individual decisions and purposes within the context of the wider story of God's people, raising such questions as: Who is the genuine builder of the temple? What are its proper foundations? What is the true nature of God's victory? Who will be the one to achieve the victory of God's people? These are questions of shared purpose.

Of course, we continue to find this dynamic interaction of personal calling and collective purpose within churches and other organizations now. An interesting example is provided by Daniel Cable in his book *Alive at Work*, where he discusses the role of purpose in contemporary organizations and how it needs to be felt rather than merely explained. He observes: 'Simply telling someone the purpose of their work is like telling them about a good book you have read. Even if it *is* good, they probably won't recommend it to one of their friends until they read it themselves and experience it firsthand' (Cable, 2018, p. 147 – emphasis original). Cable says that he frequently illustrates this principle in his teaching with a story about how fundraising for university scholarships was improved markedly by using students who had been supported by those scholarships. They were able to make the purpose of the fund much more real when explaining it to others.

Cable was sharing this story with a group of leaders for a major pharmaceutical company and one of them called out, 'I just saw this happen last year!' She was working in the medical devices division, where the morale of the team was low, partly because their work was perceived as not being held in high esteem within the wider business. One day the divisional leader brought in a customer who had diabetes and she shared her experience of how the group's work had greatly improved her life by inventing a little finger-pricking device. The whole team was affected by this patient's testimonial and for months afterwards they were motivated to work harder and better.

Naturally, Cable was encouraged by this story that supported his argument. Then another leader on the other side of the room interjected, 'Yea, they tried that bullshit on us too.' And he continued:

> I have this boss who has never talked about anything but quarterly profits and hitting shipping targets. He must have been to hear you talk about those scholarships because one day he drags a patient into our weekly meeting and makes her tell us this story of how the drugs saved her life. I mean, trying to exploit our emotions to make us work harder? Using a patient to manipulate us!? That's pretty low. (pp. 149–50)

What Cable took away from those encounters was that it not only matters *what* leaders do but also *why* they are doing it.

With respect to increasing a sense of purpose through connecting employees with their customers, some may perceive that as inspirational and moving, while others can see it as calculating or manipulative. This takes us back to the story about Jesus' question for his disciples at Caesarea Philippi and our discussion about authenticity. Cable concluded from his encounters with leaders at the pharmaceutical company:

> If a leader's purpose-building events are seen as authentic – consistent with what the leader really cares about – then the effect can be inspirational ... However, if employees think that a leader has just learned a new trick to get more out of them, the identical event can backfire. Employees can feel manipulated, disgusted, and demotivated. (Cable, 2018, p. 150)

Of course, as followers of Jesus we are not 'employees' who are seeking to connect with our 'customers'. But neither should we be seen in a literalistic understanding of Jesus' parable as workers on a building site constructing a tower or troops going into battle. However, we can use all these categories as analogies to discover more about purpose and how that can work in the context of the way in which churches function and how kingdom stories work.

Kingdom stories and purpose

What is the purpose of the Church? Different forms of ministry will have different purposes according to their context. For instance, a ministry offered in the context of a prison chaplaincy will be different from that of a church serving a new housing estate. The same is true about all aspects of church life, such as the stories we tell and the practical theology that we use. In his discussion about theology, A. Scott Moreau makes this sharply observed comment:

It is fair to say that the theology written on an empty stomach or when under observation by security forces will have an entirely different orientation from theology written in a climate-controlled office in which the most important pressure is the need to get a manuscript to the publisher by the deadline. (Moreau, 2018, p. 208)

In other words, the purpose of a church and the stories that convey that purpose will be inextricably linked to its context.

Moreau goes on to describe the storied nature of context in this way:

We tell stories of heroism, sacrifice, adventure, coming of age, redemption, and love (romantic and friendship). We admire and try to emulate those we see as heroes; we try to avoid the mistakes of those who fall short. We rely on a repertoire of stories that we learned while growing up, stories from family, friends, religious leaders, teachers, and so on. The underlying ideals grow deep roots in our hearts and enable us to define the themes that in many ways drive us. Helping new Christ-followers become embedded in the story arc of the Bible in contextual ways is a critical component of cross-cultural ministry. (pp. 230–1)

The kingdom stories that a church shares will come from a deep narrative aquifer containing many different styles of story that arise from many different sources, and how we use and retell them will depend on how see the Church's purpose (Roberts, 2014).

In addition, the ways in which these stories are heard or understood can also be crucial to how purpose is perceived. For example, in Cable's account, the responses to his use of research into fundraising for university scholarships produced diametrically opposite reactions – one that affirmed the point he was making and a story that contradicted it. As well as being intimately shaped by context, purpose is also directly related to authenticity.

But what of Jesus' kingdom story about someone planning to build a tower and a king preparing for a war? Is this a generalized parable about the importance of planning for matters relating to God's kingdom, or is it a more personalized story in which Jesus places himself at the heart of the narrative? Certainly this second reading opens up a fascinating interpretation of the parable, which is based on Perrin's understanding of Jesus' self-identification as the true, eschatological priest of the Jerusalem Temple. In this process of interpretation, we can see how context (Jewish temple faith) shapes purpose (Jesus as true high priest), which is manifested in a parable (Jesus as builder/king). The same will be true for contemporary churches in their differing forms of ministry, whether that's in a place of education, a suburban church or inner city – context shapes purpose, which results in new kingdom stories.

Prayer

Gracious God, rule in our hearts
that we may build on your foundations
as we seek your purposes in our lives
and for those places where we serve,
that we shall be guided to proclaim your kingdom of hope for
    all creation;
we ask this through the true High Priest, Jesus Christ. Amen.

On reflection

1 What is the context, or what are the contexts, in which you are offering ministry?
2 How does that affect your ministry in positive and negative ways?
3 What do you currently find inspirational and what do you find manipulative in your present situation?

7 Kingdom stories, wisdom and meaning

Let anyone with ears listen (Matthew 11.2–19)

When John heard in prison what the Messiah was doing, he sent word by his disciples and said to him, 'Are you the one who is to come, or are we to wait for another?' Jesus answered them, 'Go and tell John what you hear and see: the blind receive their sight, the lame walk, the lepers are cleansed, the deaf hear, the dead are raised, and the poor have good news brought to them. And blessed is anyone who takes no offence at me.'

As they went away, Jesus began to speak to the crowds about John: 'What did you go out into the wilderness to look at? A reed shaken by the wind? What then did you go out to see? Someone dressed in soft robes? Look, those who wear soft robes are in royal palaces. What then did you go out to see? A prophet? Yes, I tell you, and more than a prophet. This is the one about whom it is written,

"See, I am sending my messenger ahead of you,
    who will prepare your way before you."

Truly I tell you, among those born of women no one has arisen greater than John the Baptist; yet the least in the kingdom of heaven is greater than he. From the days of John the Baptist until now the kingdom of heaven has suffered violence, and the violent take it by force. For all the prophets and the law prophesied until John came; and if you are willing to accept it, he is Elijah who is to come. Let anyone with ears listen!

But to what will I compare this generation? It is like children sitting in the market-places and calling to one another,

"We played the flute for you, and you did not dance;
    we wailed, and you did not mourn."

For John came neither eating nor drinking, and they say, "He has a demon"; the Son of Man came eating and drinking, and they say, "Look, a glutton and a drunkard, a friend of tax-collectors and sinners!" Yet wisdom is vindicated by her deeds.'

This tantalizing account from Matthew's Gospel seems to focus on the question, 'Who is this?', yet at the same time shies away from clear answers. John the Baptist asks Jesus, 'Who are you?' Jesus asks the crowd, 'Who was John the Baptist?' And we are left asking, 'Who are the children sitting in the marketplaces?'

Jesus' reply to John's disciples is not to acknowledge openly that he is the Messiah but to point to signs of the kingdom and draw upon the language of Isaiah (26.19; 29.18; 35.5–6; 42.7, 18; 61.1) and suggest that in his actions those prophecies are being fulfilled. Then, in the language of satire with references to reeds shaken by the wind and people dressed in soft robes, Jesus provides a clearer response to his rhetorical question about John the Baptist. Who is he? He is Elijah. But even that straightforward statement has significant unspoken implications: let anyone with ears listen! And who are the children calling in the marketplaces? Some see them as Jesus and John, but others have argued they are the publicans and sinners. We need the gift of wisdom to understand all that is happening in this kingdom narrative.

Wisdom has long been a treasured resource. It is associated with leadership and aspiration in ancient Greek thinking and through much of the Hebrew Bible. Wisdom was valued throughout Mediterranean and Middle Eastern cultures, particularly in the royal courts and centres of learning. It is a multifaceted phenomenon, which includes insight and interpretation. Michael Sadgrove puts it in this way:

Interpretation lies at the heart of wisdom, for in its manifestations, wisdom is always a way of looking at reality that finds patterns, connections and meanings ... biblical wisdom is shot through with the vocabulary and imagery of 'seeing'. Having 'insight', 'perception' or 'illumination' are among the gifts that characterize the wise who 'see' in the ways that casual observers fail to do. (Sadgrove, 2008, p. 40)

That is what is happening in this kingdom story and Jesus' use of these 'Who is this?' questions. He is asking John's disciples, the crowd and all who are listening to have an insight beyond that of a casual observer and to discern the patterns and deeper meanings of all that is happening around them. That is the profound challenge that kingdom stories present, then as now.

David Hurst, a writer and speaker on organizations and management, has made a similar point when he contends that 'The making of meaning is the primary role of leadership in every organization. Meaning is made by distilling experience; we call the resulting essence "wisdom"' (Hurst, 2012, p. 3). He goes on to argue that one of the most powerful ways in which humanity sets about organizing and communicating this distilled experience is through narrative or meaningful story:

Humankind has used this medium for thousands of years, and its value to our survival as a species has been immense. It is still the primary way in which we make sense of cause and effect in our own lives and the organizations and communities with which are involved. (p. 8)

In *The New Ecology of Leadership* (2012), Hurst sets out what he calls the infinity-shaped ecocycle for understanding organizational change (pp. 46–8). The front loop of the eco-cycle describes the journey of business from conception through growth and maturity to decline and crisis. The back loop presents a less well-known journey moving from crisis to renewal. What is of particular interest for our purposes now are the images, language and narrative that Hurst uses for that second journey, from the edge of disaster to restoration.

The story that Hurst narrates is of a mid-sized North

American industrial distributor based in Toronto called Hugh Russel Inc., and the language he uses is all drawn from the Old Testament. As a member of the company throughout this period of crisis, he is drawing on his own detailed experience. The story begins with a successful take-over bid for Hugh Russel from a company that could not then cope with a looming financial crisis and left everyone at the mercy of their creditors. Some highly motivated employees were able to put Hugh Russel on a sound financial footing and provide new vision for the company, which meant it could go its separate way from the company that had taken it over.

Interestingly this three-stage transition from crisis to renewal is told by Hurst as a version of the Exodus story. When Hugh Russel is taken over it is plunged into the wilderness where the Hebrews roam after their escape from Egypt. From this place of confusion, creative leadership emerges, which Hurst sees as a process of climbing the mountain to see the promised land. The final stage is entering into the land through the leadership of those who take the innovative decisions needed for the company.

We might argue that such an approach is only to be expected in a North American context where the stories and language of the Bible still hold currency. However, I would say that Hurst is correct to observe that something broader is happening when narratives from all cultures are taken up and reworked. He states:

> story and metaphor are the medium of leadership – it is the way in which *homo sapiens* has made sense of complexity for thousands of years, and today it is still the way in which leaders make meaning for people and define their organization's reality. (Hurst, 2012, p. 97)

This relates back to the point made in the previous chapter about context. The renewed vision and restored purpose of this firm has been retold through a story that makes sense in its context. If the business had been based in Singapore or

India, for example, different stories may have been to hand, and it is perfectly possible that other narratives can be used in this way. Aesop's fables, Shakespeare's plays, Hans Christian Andersen's fairy tales, Kipling's Just-so tales all continue to have a narrative power and provide stories that human beings use in our meaning-making.

However, it is important to introduce a note of caution here, because there is a danger that 'meaning' can be trivialized to the point of being meaningless. One of the leading thinkers who established the importance of meaning was Victor Frankl, a Jewish survivor of the Nazi concentration camp at Auschwitz. From that dreadful experience of suffering he concluded that personal meaning was the one thing that was dependable: 'Meaning was the irreducible core of our human being, which could never be taken away. For Frankl, meaning was found through the struggle for life, through the deprivation of virtually all other human needs' (Walker, 2011, p. 173). With these thoughts in mind, we turn back to our kingdom story from Matthew 11 and explore its ongoing meaning for ministry.

Wisdom and kingdom stories

The Greek word for wisdom (*sophia*) occurs sparingly in the Gospels – not at all in John, once in Mark, three times in Matthew and six in Luke. By comparison it occurs 28 times in the Pauline letters. Nevertheless, the impact of wisdom terminology has been identified as an important element in early Christian understandings of Jesus in the New Testament and elsewhere. James D. G. Dunn's comprehensive five-chapter summary is still well worth reading (Dunn, 1980). But more specifically, what about its role in the teasing parable that we have before us?

There is another version of this story in Luke's Gospel (7.31–35), where perhaps the most striking difference is in the conclusion when the Third Evangelist writes: 'Nevertheless, wisdom is vindicated by her children.' The eminent New

Testament scholar Martin Hengel believes that these words are more likely to be original because Matthew's version, which ends with the word 'works', is very typical of his writing (Hengel, 2004, pp. 80–1). I do not believe that it matters much for our purposes here whether Jesus said 'children' or 'works' because what is key is the 'vindication' of wisdom.

If we look again at Hurst's use of the Exodus narrative in creating meaning for his twenty-first-century company in the midst of a crisis, we can see something similar taking place in Jesus' use of Isaiah and Elijah for his first-century listeners. There is a crisis for God's people, which should be obvious from reading Isaiah's words and hearing about Elijah's story. If people have the wisdom then they can see how renewal of God's people and the restoration of God kingdom will be achieved, but little heed is being taken of God's messengers in the here and now of Jesus' time.

There has been the music of dancing and celebration (Jesus), together with the music of lamentation and mourning (John the Baptist), yet no one has responded because they do not have the wisdom to understand the meaning in the kingdom stories of both Jesus and John. For the most part those who saw and heard the Son of Man and the Baptist remained passive observers and did not involve themselves in the story that was unfolding before them.

Ruth Etchells warns bluntly that the same beguiling temptation can exist in our own world. She writes about this passage:

> So we do not join in the divine Game, and instead sit carping on the side. Not recognising that this Game is the name of reality, the only reality there is: and that if we are not alert to it, ready to take part in it, and so fail to join the Game, it will pass us by and others will be drawn into it. And leave us, at the end, with no Game to play. (Etchells, 1998, pp. 105–6)

In other words, the same challenge remains for us as it did for Jesus' original hearers. Are we going to hear the music? Will we have the wisdom to recognize the seriousness of God's 'game' and encourage others to join the dance of the kingdom and tell their stories about taking to the floor in order to discover wisdom and meaning? We shall return to the theme of wisdom and kingdom stories at the start of Chapter 4.

Prayer

God of all wisdom and knowledge,
we are your children,
so we pray that we may always be attentive to your voice
when you call us to join in the dance of your kingdom;
that in our encounters with your Spirit
we may be granted true understanding and sound judgement;
we ask this through the One who is your Eternal Word. Amen.

On reflection

1 Where do you find personal wisdom for your ministry?
2 Where do you find organizational wisdom for church ministry?
3 Where do you find shared wisdom for those with whom you are involved in the Body of Christ?

8 Kingdom stories and discipleship

Parable of the talents (Matthew 25.14-30)

[Jesus said to his disciples, 'The kingdom of heaven] is as if a man, going on a journey, summoned his slaves and entrusted his property to them; to one he gave five talents, to another two, to another one, to each according to his ability. Then he went away. The one who had received the five talents went off at once and traded with them, and made five more talents. In the same way, the one who had the two talents made two more talents. But the one who had received the one talent went off and dug a hole in the ground and hid his master's money. After a long time the master of those slaves came and settled accounts with them. Then the one who had received the five talents came forward, bringing five more talents, saying, "Master, you handed over to me five talents; see, I have made five more talents." His master said to him, "Well done, good and trustworthy slave; you have been trustworthy in a few things, I will put you in charge of many things; enter into the joy of your master." And the one with the two talents also came forward, saying, "Master, you handed over to me two talents; see, I have made two more talents." His master said to him, "Well done, good and trustworthy slave; you have been trustworthy in a few things, I will put you in charge of many things; enter into the joy of your master." Then the one who had received the one talent also came forward, saying, "Master, I knew that you were a harsh man, reaping where you did not sow, and gathering where you did not scatter seed; so I was afraid, and I went and hid your talent in the ground. Here you have what is yours." But his master replied, "You wicked and lazy slave! You knew, did you, that I reap where I did not sow, and gather where I did not scatter? Then you ought to have invested my money with the bankers, and on my return I would have received what was my own with interest. So take the talent from him, and give it to the one with the ten talents. For to all those who have, more will be given,

> and they will have an abundance; but from those who have noth-
> ing, even what they have will be taken away. As for this worthless
> slave, throw him into the outer darkness, where there will be
> weeping and gnashing of teeth."'

In *The Leader's Guide to Storytelling*, Stephen Denning begins
by offering a historical perspective on storytelling and how it
relates to our contemporary world. Thus, he argues:

> The stories that are most effective in a modern organization
> do not necessarily follow the rules laid down in Aristotle's
> *Poetics*. They often reflect an ancient but different tradition
> of storytelling in a minimalist fashion, which is reflected in
> the parables of the Bible and European folk tales. (Denning,
> 2011, p. 8)

One of the parables he goes on to quote is popularly known as
Jesus' parable of the talents, from Matthew 25.14–30.

After citing that parable in full, Denning goes on to make a
more generalized point about how such narratives work:

> A parable begins with a narrative imagining – the understand-
> ing of a complex of objects, events, actors and objectives as
> organized by a story. It then combines story with projection
> – one story is projected onto another. The parable of talents
> might be projected onto various activities – the effort to be
> a better person, the investment of money, the education of
> children, or the launching of a change program in an organ-
> ization. (p. 144)

Before we set out how a 'narrative imagining' from the parable
of the talents might work as a kingdom story in churches today,
we need to explore how it can be understood in its historical
context. To this end I shall draw upon two different interpretations offered by T. W. Manson and N. T. Wright, which go

some way to illustrating Denning's point about how contrasting conclusions and lessons can be drawn from the same story.

In *The Sayings of Jesus*, Manson describes how he sees this parable in terms of a principle set out in the Torah but not expressly stated in Jesus' words, that slaves belong to their owners so anything slaves produce or earn also belongs to those owners. The theological conclusion drawn from this legal tenet is that the purpose of human existence is to serve God, and all that we have belongs to God. In addition: 'The reward of such service is opportunity for further and larger service; and the worst punishment for failure to serve is just to be deprived of the opportunity to serve at all' (Manson, 1949, p. 245).

For Manson, the parable reaches its conclusion in verse 29 with Jesus' statement, 'For to all those who have, more will be given, and they will have an abundance; but from those who have nothing, even what they have will be taken away.' In other words, the work of God's kingdom goes on and the task that one disciple fails to discharge is given to another who will do it properly and thoroughly.

Wright also sees the parable in terms of the accountability of the servants left in charge of the property, but in *Jesus and the Victory of God* he places the story in a very different interpretive framework by asking, 'Who is the king and who are the servants here?' However, rather than seeing the departing king as Jesus and the remaining subjects as the Church, Wright suggests this is about YHWH returning to visit God's people in Jerusalem (Zion). A key element is where we place ourselves in the process of 'narrative imagining'.

In this approach to the parable, what Wright calls the ideal hearer 'is located near the end of the story, when the master is about to return. This fits with the emphasis of Jesus' entire public career: the moment that counts is even now upon us. YHWH is now at last visiting his people' (Wright, 1996, pp. 637–8). Taking this line, the returning king is Jesus who is embodying God's return to Zion and bringing judgement upon those who had been left in charge of YHWH's people – some of whom had been faithful, whereas others had been negligent.

This return of the king was then enacted by Jesus when he rode into Jerusalem on a donkey and pronounced God's judgement in the Temple courtyard upon those servants who were unfit and deficient in their service of the kingdom.

If we place Wright and Manson's interpretations together we have a parable that in its first narrative imagining has Jesus speaking judgement upon those religious leaders who were overseeing the work of the Temple and therefore the religious life of God's people. In Matthew's subsequent narrative imagining, that application has been widened to encompass the people of God within the Body of Christ – those who are now seeking to walk in the way of Christ.

We have already considered the nature of followership and being called by Jesus, but the notion of discipleship takes us deeper into what it means to be a follower of Christ. As David Brown has said: 'discipleship, if it is about anything, is surely not so much about instantaneous results as about a continuing process of transformation, as both as individuals and as a community we gradually learn more deeply of God's meaning and purpose for our lives' (Brown, 2000, p. 406). The parable of the talents is a kingdom story about discipleship as an ongoing process of stewardship and transformation. One of the consistent challenges set by this parable is how we take the gifts given to us by God and continuously use them in the service of the kingdom.

Kingdom stories and discipleship

Gerd Theissen provides a really succinct summary for the whole of Matthew 25 when he writes that, for the readers of this Gospel, 'Constant watchfulness is demanded (25.1–13), as well as the use of the gifts that have been entrusted to each (25.14–30) and helpfulness towards every sister and brother (25.31–46)' (Theissen, 1992, p. 274). That, in turn, is a helpful primer for Christian discipleship. One of the dangers being warned against specifically in the parable of the talents is of individuals and communities not properly using their God-given abilities. This is well illustrated by this kingdom story from the American preacher Fred Craddock.

Some years ago there was a new minister who, having finished his training went to serve a little church in what was a small town experiencing massive growth. Everywhere seemed to be a building site; constructors were living in caravans and everyone appeared to be wearing a hard-hat as they laboured to build houses, shops and the other things needed for a growing community. And the new minister's church was close to all this activity. It was a beautiful little church – old and picturesque. It had an organ which one of the young-sters had to pump by hand; it was beautifully decorated and lit by carefully tended paraffin lamps; and every pew in this little church had been hand-carved from trees that had grown nearby. This was the place the young minister was going to begin his vocation, his calling from God; and – not long after he'd started – he asked the leaders to stay behind one Sunday and said to them, 'We need to reach out amongst all those caravans and invite those people to church.'

'Oh, I don't know. I don't think they'd fit in,' said one person. 'They're only here temporarily, just construction people,' said another. 'They'll be leaving pretty soon.'

'But we ought to invite them, make them feel at home,' the new minister said. They continued to debate the matter, time ran out and they decided to vote next Sunday. Next Sunday came and everyone sat down after the service. 'I move,' said one person, 'I move that in order to belong to this church you must own property in the town.' Someone else said, 'I second that.' The young minister voted against, but the motion passed.

By and by, the young minister was called to serve another church. He got married and raised a family. Eventually he was in the neighbourhood again and he took his wife to see the beautiful old church with the hand-pumped organ, the neat paraffin lamps and ... the painful memory. It was a challenge but, finally, they found it off a new motorway, down a road, along a gravel track and amongst some pine trees. It was still there but different. There was a car park full of motorbikes, cars and four-wheel drives and a sign saying: All You Can Eat. It was now a restaurant. They went inside. The hand-carved pews were against the wall and there were now electric lights. People were eating at polished tables. 'All kinds of people,' thought the minister, 'Parthians, Medes, Edomites and dwellers of Mesopotamia. Yes ... All kinds of people.' And the old minister – who'd once been the young minister – said to his wife, 'Well, it's a good thing this isn't still a church, otherwise these people – they couldn't be in here.' (Craddock, 2001, pp. 28–9; adapted)

The local church leaders in that story did not recognize the signs of the kingdom and therefore did not utilize their God-given gifts in its service. Craddock's reference to the 'Parthians, Medes, Edomites and dwellers of Mesopotamia' locates the story in Acts 2 and Jesus' disciples receiving the Holy Spirit on the day of Pentecost. There was a lack of narrative imagination in the little church, which is a challenge for any church at any time and in any context.

Returning to Denning's use of story in all forms of organization, he believes that:

A parable affords an infinite number of applications, as different readers or listeners use projection from the base story to imagine a new story in their own contexts. As a result, a parable tends to have great longevity: the parables of the Bible are still going strong, some two thousand years after they were created. (2011, p. 144)

Discipleship requires us to nurture that narrative imagination which was lacking in the church that was turned into a diner. Kingdom stories ask us to seek out and be watchful for signs of God's activity in our world and not to be negligent in how we use our talents in God's service.

Prayer

O God of Life,
you sustain us with the generosity of your love;
bring us to that heavenly banquet
where your table is open to strangers and pilgrims
called by your Holy Spirit;
we ask this in the name of Christ, the bread for all. Amen.

On reflection

1 In what ways is good discipleship and stewardship being exercised in churches, congregations and groups of which you are a member?

2 Where could that discipleship and stewardship be improved?

3 In what ways are you exercising narrative imagination in terms of discipleship?

9 Kingdom stories and trust

Jesus washes the disciples' feet (John 13.2–16)

> During supper Jesus, knowing that the Father had given all things into his hands, and that he had come from God and was going to God, got up from the table, took off his outer robe, and tied a towel around himself. Then he poured water into a basin and began to wash the disciples' feet and to wipe them with the towel that was tied around him. He came to Simon Peter, who said to him, 'Lord, are you going to wash my feet?' Jesus answered, 'You do not know now what I am doing, but later you will understand.' Peter said to him, 'You will never wash my feet.' Jesus answered, 'Unless I wash you, you have no share with me.' Simon Peter said to him, 'Lord, not my feet only but also my hands and my head!' Jesus said to him, 'One who has bathed does not need to wash, except for the feet, but is entirely clean. And you are clean, though not all of you.' For he knew who was to betray him; for this reason he said, 'Not all of you are clean.'
>
> After he had washed their feet, had put on his robe, and had returned to the table, he said to them, 'Do you know what I have done to you? You call me Teacher and Lord – and you are right, for that is what I am. So if I, your Lord and Teacher, have washed your feet, you also ought to wash one another's feet. For I have set you an example, that you also should do as I have done to you. Very truly, I tell you, servants are not greater than their master, nor are messengers greater than the one who sent them.'

John's account of Jesus washing his disciples' feet is a conundrum. It is a vivid and powerful story that is found nowhere else in the Gospel accounts. The Fourth Evangelist places it within the context of his retelling of the Last Supper, which notably omits the breaking of bread and sharing of wine. Furthermore, it is deeply characteristic of the way in which the Fourth Evangelist recounts events. The ambiguous dialogue between Jesus and Peter is typical of John's Gospel. Yet the story also contains elements that run throughout the Jesus traditions, not least the saying, 'Very truly, I tell you, servants are not greater than their master, nor are messengers greater than the one who sent them.'

There is a striking parallel in Luke's Gospel. After Jesus has said the words of institution at the Last Supper a dispute breaks out among the disciples about who is the greatest. Jesus intervenes with some observations about how authority is abused by those in power, and he draws a sharp contrast regarding how it should be in God's kingdom when he says:

'But not so with you; rather the greatest among you must become like the youngest, and the leader like one who serves. For who is greater, the one who is at the table or the one who serves? Is it not the one at the table? But I am among you as one who serves.' (Luke 22.26–27)

The similarities between John's story of the foot-washing and Luke's account of the dispute about authority, both in the upper room, have suggested to some commentators that there is a direct link here. However, C. H. Dodd noted how Jesus' teaching about servanthood is found in different forms across various strands in the Gospels and draws a different conclusion. He argues:

In all, the saying in various forms appears six times in the Synoptic Gospels. Whatever may be the truth about the tangled literary interrelations of these several passages, it seems clear that a maxim to this effect held a position of particular importance in the tradition of the sayings of the Lord, and entered into several different formulations of his teaching. (Dodd, 1976, p. 61)

While historians may debate the precise connection between John's foot-washing narrative and Luke's account of the dispute about authority, we can be confident that Jesus used servanthood as a model for leadership in his proclamation of God's kingdom.

This is deeply embedded in the symbolic act of washing feet. According to Jewish tradition, people were expected to wash the dust of the streets from their feet before approaching the sacred precincts of the Temple. N. T. Wright suggests that this act of foot-washing could be seen as placing the events of the Last Supper as part of Jesus' counter-Temple narrative. The true Temple was being gathered and enacted in that place and time (Wright, 1996, p. 558). It is natural to start to explore this action in terms of servanthood and in terms of the suffering servant from the prophecy of Isaiah. But there is another way to look at this kingdom story and we get a clue in Dodd's observation that Jesus' foot-washing has also to be seen within a first-century Jewish culture in which it was a mark of exceptional deference (Dodd, 1968, p. 401). We could see this as a display of humility but it could be that in the context of the Last Supper, Jesus is also seeking to be a good host.

In his writing about undefended leadership, Simon P. Walker contends that leading is about the space between leaders and followers, or more precisely the relationships that are being created and managed. He suggests that if we think of leadership as being not heroic or a servant, but as being a host, then we should think in terms of the space that is being created for the group. Thus:

> You can't think about a host without thinking about a party, or a home, to which guests are welcomed. You start to think about the relationships that already exist, the friendships that may be formed. You start to think about leadership in terms of encounter and conversation. (Walker, 2011, p. 378)

The role of 'host' recurs throughout Jesus' public ministry and teaching. There are times when he is the host, such as at the Last Supper and the miraculous feedings.

There are times when he is hosted by some notorious members of the local community – for example, Levi (Luke 5.27–32) and Zacchaeus (Luke 19.1–10), who were tax collectors, and Simon who had leprosy (Mark 14.3–9). And being a host features in his parables – such as the great banquet (Matthew 22.1–14) and the conclusion to the parable of the prodigal son (Luke 15.11–32). As Sam Wells has noted, 'The heavenly banquet is perhaps the most characteristic scriptural depiction of the life of the kingdom. Jesus enacts these banquets himself in his many significant meals with sinners, strangers, crowds and disciples. These are invitations to join the inner-communion of God' (Wells, 2006, p. 42).

Once we begin to think of leading as an activity that involves such encounters then we need to ask what facilitates such human interaction, engagement and meeting. I would argue that a crucial element in this process is developing trust. We have already touched on this in the discussion about risk and, like risk, this is not a word that occurs very often in the Gospels or in Jesus' kingdom stories, but it can be seen frequently in the accounts of his symbolic deeds and actions, of which the foot-washing is a good example. Within his cultural context Jesus is seeking to be a good host and to model a form of leadership that is deeply rooted within the traditions and stories about him. He does this by enacting a form of kingdom authority and through continuing to build trust among the disciples as his own story reaches its moment of crisis with his arrest and crucifixion.

There has been some interesting research on trust in various contemporary organizations, commissioned by the Chartered Institute of Personnel and Development (CIPD) from the University of Bath, which has drawn upon (among others) the Church of England. The first research report (*Cultivating Trustworthy Leaders*, 2014a) sets out an ecosystem of trust that explores four types or drivers of trustworthiness: (i) Emphasizing ability; (ii) Emphasizing benevolence; (iii) Emphasizing integrity; (iv) Emphasizing predictability. This is summarized in Figure 2.1.

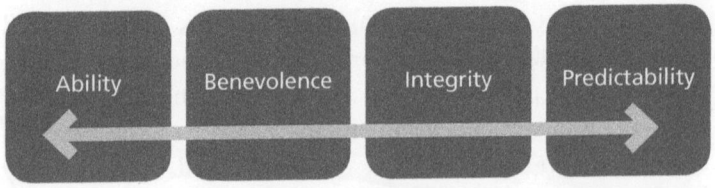

Figure 2.1: Drivers of trustworthiness (Dietz and Den Hartog, 2006)

These terms are defined in the following ways. Ability describes perceptions of leadership competence in leaders doing their job or fulfilling their role. Benevolence describes a concern for others beyond leaders' own needs and showing levels of care and compassion. Integrity defines how trustworthiness is linked to being seen as someone who adheres to principles of fairness and honesty while avoiding hypocrisy. Predictability emphasizes how leadership behaviour has to be consistent over time (2014a, p. 2).[1]

The second research report (*Experiencing Trustworthy Leadership*, 2014b) argues that trust-building involves those involved in leading in the following categories of behaviour: (i) Behavioural consistency; (ii) Behavioural integrity; (iii) Sharing and delegation of control; (iv) Communication; (v) Demonstration of concern; (vi) Consulting team members when making decisions; (vii) Communicating a collective vision; (viii) Exhibiting shared values. The report summarizes this approach in four underpinning themes set out in Figure 2.2.

We can see some of these dynamics at work in Jesus' kingdom stories and actions. Sometimes they manifest themselves in obvious ways but at other times they are less transparent, and the story of the foot-washing provides examples of both. For instance, take leadership ability. Jesus has led the 12 disciples to Jerusalem and to the upper room, but not without a degree of resistance and opposition. As the story of Christ's passion makes clear, Jesus is fulfilling his role even while those around him are unclear about what that role is. Something similar could be said to be at work as far as predictability is concerned. Ever since the question Jesus asked of his disciples at Caesarea Philippi (Chapter 2.5), he has been consistent in knowing that

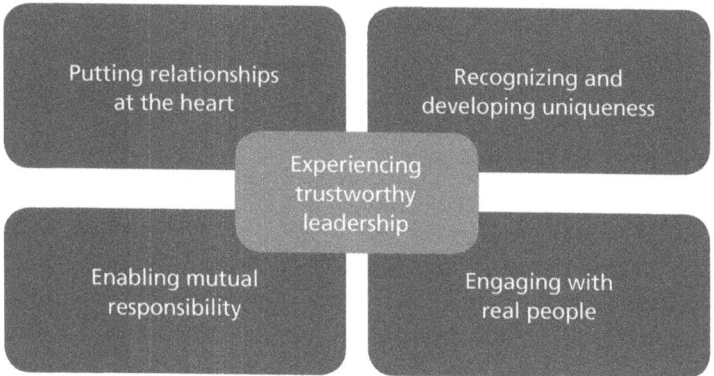

Figure 2.2: Experiencing trustworthy leadership

the destiny of God's kingdom lies in Jerusalem. The disciples have had consistent confidence in Jesus' ability to lead them to the capital, the Temple and the upper room, even if what they envisaged happening in Jerusalem appeared to bear little resemblance to what took place. Jesus has been leading and has been consistent, even if those who were following were not certain about the ultimate destination.

By contrast, the simple action of taking up a basin, water and towel enacts the care and compassion of Jesus, in this instance as a host. Within this culture there is an expectation that such an action is part of the welcome. And this is linked to a sense of integrity and a lack of hypocrisy. The symbolic washing of feet is a powerful way of showing humility and building trust. Of course, there are other levels of symbolism too, such as baptism, which are alluded to in the dialogue between Jesus and Peter. It is also worth noting that towards the start of Jesus' ministry in John's Gospel there is a story about purification rites and water at the wedding in Cana (John 2.1–11). The contrast between the abundance of water and wine at the wedding with the basin of water and the cup of wine in the upper room is a reminder of Sam Wells' observation that 'the embodiment of perfect service, of the abundance of God, of freedom in obedience, is Jesus. His relationship with the Father is the epitome of perfect service. This is true in circumstances of scarcity as much as in circumstances of abundance' (Wells, 2006, p. 37).

Kingdom stories and trust

To conclude our discussion of kingdom stories and trust, let me begin with two contrasting tales about being a host. One of Aesop's fables is about a lion, fox and donkey who'd successfully acquired a large amount of food. So the lion asked the donkey to divide up their prize. Carefully, the donkey divided up the spoil into three equal shares. However, the lion was offended, burst into a violent rage and then devoured the donkey!

Next, the lion asked the fox to make a division. The fox accumulated all they'd killed into one large heap and left but a small morsel for himself. The lion said, 'This is perfect. Who taught you how to divide so well?'

The fox replied, 'I just recently learnt it from the donkey!'

The Jesuit theologian Anthony de Mello tells the story about a farmer whose corn always took the first prize at the state fair, and who had a habit of sharing his best corn seed with all the farmers in the neighbourhood. A newcomer to the area was puzzled by this action, so he asked the farmer why he did this. 'Well,' replied the prize-winner, 'it's really a matter of my own interests. The wind picks up the pollen and carries it from field to field. So if my neighbours grow inferior corn the cross-pollination brings down the quality of my own corn. That's why I am concerned that they plant only the very best' (de Mello, 1989, p. 173).

The disparity on the place of trust and teamwork in those two stories is pointed. In Aesop's parable the donkey trusted the lion and paid the price, so the fox learns what collaboration truly means in that team, where subservience and obedience are fundamental. Whereas in the second story, teamwork is based partly on self-interest, but that is shared by all the characters and so is at least a step in the right direction. I would argue that any encounter with trust and any story (or any research report, for that matter) that builds trust is a kingdom story. We see from the account of Jesus washing his disciples' feet that such stories embody a crucial kingdom value – that of trust. And we can see too from research into contemporary organizations that this value is vital to the way in which healthy communities, businesses and churches function.

Prayer

O God of trust and service,
we offer heartfelt thanks for our Lord Jesus Christ
who came not to be served but to serve;
be with each of us as we are ordained to proclaim your kingdom
and reveal your love for our broken world,
in the sacrifice of our living saviour,
Jesus Christ our Lord. Amen.

On reflection

1 How is trust nurtured in the churches and organizations of which you are a part?
2 Are there other categories of behaviour that you think are important for trust-building?
3 What behaviours, if any, are presently undermining trust in groups to which you belong?

Note

1 For further discussion around issues of trust in organizations, see R. C. Mayer, J. H. Davis and D. Schoorman, 1995, 'An Integrative Model of Organizational Trust', *Academy of Management Review*, 20:3, pp. 709–34; Graham Dietz and Deanne N. Den Hartog, 2006, 'Measuring Trust inside Organizations', *Personnel Review*, 35:5, pp. 557–88.

10 Jesus and kingdom stories: conclusion

In this chapter we have explored how we can see signs of God's kingdom in the Gospel stories told about Jesus and how they relate to our contemporary world. At one level this is a straightforward process. The Gospels can be seen as a form of biography (Burridge, 2004) but, in his discussion of the Bible, John Barton notes the way in which each of the evangelists highlights particular themes and at certain points different chronologies: 'These differing emphases imply that the evangelists were creative writers, not merely transcribers or compilers' (Barton, 2019, p. 208). Barton goes on to argue that this narrative plurality is often overlooked by the churches but that this diversity is fundamental to Christian practice and ministry.

These four writers were telling the story of Jesus from their perspective and the outlook of the early Christian communities that they were writing for. However, their task was even more complex than it first appears. They were seeking to record and pass on a narrative that is inherently paradoxical. As we saw in Chapter 1, Jesus' proclamation of God's kingdom was both imminent and transcendent. In other words, that which is 'of God' can be seen breaking into the 'present moment' for those who had eyes to see and ears to hear such things. This had implications for Jesus' immediate followers and it has implications for us as well. As Nicholas Perrin observes: 'The paradoxical nature of Jesus' vocation in turn sets the pattern for the paradoxical experience of those who would participate in his in-breaking kingdom' (Perrin, 2018, p. 288).

This chapter has begun to explore ways in which our stories can encounter stories about Jesus and God's kingdom. This is what I mean by an engaged eschatology – being alive to God's action in our present world and God's involvement with the tales that we are telling. For me, something of the paradoxical and ephemeral nature of kingdom stories is reflected in Ann Lewin's poem entitled 'Disclosure':

Prayer is like watching for the
Kingfisher. All you can do is
Be where he is likely to appear, and
Wait.
Often, nothing much happens;
There is space, silence and
Expectancy.
No visible sign, only the
Knowledge that he's been there,
And may come again.
Seeing or not seeing cease to matter,
You have been prepared.
But sometimes, when you've almost
Stopped expecting it,
A flash of brightness
Gives encouragement.[1]

In a similar way, kingdom stories can be flashes of brightness
that give encouragement, but they can also be something more.
By weaving our personal, family and communal stories into
those of Jesus, we are entering into Jesus' paradoxical vocation
where the transcendent nature and values of God are engaging
with the lives of others and the communities in which we are
embedded. In this chapter I have explored this in terms of eight
kingdom stories from the Gospel accounts and eight ideas
from our present-day culture (risk, followership, typologies,
authenticity, purpose, meaning/wisdom, discipleship, trust.)
This process of knowing the story of Christianity so that it
can be applied in the present day is one of the ten ideas for
leading stories in churches outlined in both *The Power of Story
to Change a Church* (2017b, pp. 24–5) and *Leading by Story*
(Roberts and Sims, 2017, pp. 183–5).

In the next chapter we shall begin to turn our attention to
two of the other ideas for leading stories in church – listening to stories about the past and listening to stories being told
in the present. More specifically, we shall be exploring where
kingdom stories can be found in the world around us – first

in narratives illustrated by past and present artistic expression (Chapter 3) and then in stories that emerge in forms of commemoration and remembrance (Chapter 4).

Note

1 Ann Lewin, 'Disclosure', in *Watching for the Kingfisher* © Ann Lewin, 2009, Canterbury Press. Used by permission; rights@hymnsam. co.uk.

3

The Church and Kingdom Stories

1 Introduction

In Chapter 2.4 we examined how typologies are a means for understanding and controlling organizational complexity. Another way of handling different forms of complexity is through simple binaries – 0 and 1 in mathematics, good and evil in ethics, leaders and managers in organization studies, competing siblings in literature, heaven and earth in theology, and such like.[1] In the same way that typologies can have both their uses and limitations, so can binaries, and the irony in that statement is intentional! There is a sense in which my concept of engaged eschatology is in essence a binary, using Thompson's poetic image, 'betwixt heaven and Charing Cross'. In this chapter I shall explore some interactions between the Church and kingdom stories through a series of binary relationships.

First, we will take the Italian artist Luca Signorelli's depiction of the Last Judgement in his frescoes for Orvieto cathedral and explore some dichotomies between earth/heaven and management/leadership, drawing upon the philosophical approach of Sverre Spoelstra. Second, we will scrutinize Henry Scott Holland's words about death being nothing at all, which has become a popular reading at funerals, although the original sermon from which they are extracted offers a binary choice between 'death is nothing at all' and death as 'the supreme irrevocable disaster'. We will explore Scott Holland's idea through a more contemporary art form – that of film. And, in particular, the films *The Shape of Water* and *Coco*. Then, in conclusion, I will consider insights from Samuel Wells on the

life and work of the German theologian Dietrich Bonhoeffer
and how they point us beyond binaries to kingdom stories.

Note

1 A third way of handling such complexity is through a set of axes
or series of binaries; for example, see Marsh and Roberts' use of acoustic axes to interpret the way in which people listen to popular music
(Marsh and Roberts, 2015), which I have extended to understanding
the sacred and profane elements in folk music (Roberts, 2017a).

2 End of times and engaged eschatology

Last Judgement comes to Orvieto

The ancient city of Orvieto is built high on a volcanic outcrop, defended by steep cliffs and lofty walls. Inside this protective shell is a striking cathedral dedicated to the Assumption of the Virgin Mary. The cathedral includes the Cappella Nuova (New Chapel), which was finished in 1444, and striking frescoes of the Last Judgement, which were begun in 1447 – originally by the early Italian Renaissance painter Fra Angelico. He was a respected Dominican theologian who, prior to being asked to undertake this commission, had turned down being Archbishop of Florence. It is thought by some that it may well have been Fra Angelico who suggested the theme of the Last Judgement.

Certainly Fra Angelico had completed an altarpiece of the Last Judgement for a convent in Florence and rendered another one after starting the New Chapel, so it seems to have been a subject that appealed to him. He develops themes of repentance and intercession in line with Thomist theology, giving a more positive and hopeful view of this subject than some medieval compositions. However, only two sections were completed by him – those of *Christ the Judge* and *Angels and Prophets*. It was over fifty years before Luca Signorelli would be contracted to complete the commission, and it is thought that he realized the designs left by Fra Angelico before working on his own pictorial compositions for the project.

As well as being an artist, Signorelli has been described as a 'poet-theologian', but his most lasting impact is in his portrayal of the human body, which greatly influenced both Michelangelo and Raphael. To put him in context, he started this project around the time Leonardo Da Vinci finished his *Last Supper* in Milan, about 1498–9. Signorelli had trained with Piero della Francesca in Arezzo and seems to have been held in high regard by commentators of the time, including Vasari, who noted that this artist played a seminal role in the formation of the High Renaissance style. Signorelli also helped to decorate the lower walls in the Sistine Chapel. However, it's worth keeping in mind that not all theologians were solely focused on the intellectual study of their subject. Stephen Langton, Archbishop of Canterbury in the thirteenth century and a principal theologian in pre-Thomist Paris, argued for reaching out to lay people through the popular sermon and, although Signorelli's work was aimed at an educated audience, it also spoke to the populous at large (James, 2003, p. 8).

Sources for the frescoes

According to Dugald McLellan, in his Orvieto frescoes Signorelli divides the story of the last days into two parts – the *Coming of the Son of Man* and the *Last Judgement* – balancing on the fulcrum of Fra Angelico's *Christ the Judge* (McLellan, 1998, p. 33). Figure 3.1 (page 89) shows Signorelli's depiction of the coming of the Son of Man, including a rendition of the Antichrist, which is unusual in Christian art. In fact, the figure of 'antichrist' is a composite character that is only named four times in the New Testament – in the First and Second Letters of John (1 John 2.18, 22; 4.3; 2 John 7). So, for instance, in 1 John 2 we read:

> Children, it is the last hour! As you have heard that antichrist is coming, so now many antichrists have come. From this we know that it is the last hour … Who is the liar but the one who denies that Jesus is the Christ? This is the antichrist, the one who denies the Father and the Son.

There's a similar theme expressed in 2 Thessalonians 2.3–4, but without the term 'antichrist':

> Let no one deceive you in any way; for that day will not come unless the rebellion comes first and the lawless one is revealed, the one destined for destruction. He opposes and

exalts himself above every so-called god or object of worship, so that he takes his seat in the temple of God, declaring himself to be God.

And we have Jesus' own apocalyptic discourses, especially in Mark 13, of which verses 5–6 are an example: 'Jesus began to say to them, "Beware that no one leads you astray. Many will come in my name and say, 'I am he!' and they will lead many astray."'

Some biblical scholars have seen the process of interpreting these words and this figure as starting within the New Testament itself, arguing that the Gospel of Luke sees the events of the Antichrist in terms of the fall of Jerusalem in 70 CE and the Gospel of John sees the Antichrist as Judas (the 'son of destruction' in John 17.12). Whether or not we see the Antichrist as a figure who has already come and gone, it is clear that for some Christians the Antichrist continues to have a contemporary relevance, and that may well have been the case at the time when Signorelli was painting his frescoes.

General influences would have included *The Golden Legend* (an imaginative 'lives of the saints' compiled in the late thirteenth century) and Dante's *Divine Comedy* (written in the early fourteenth century), but there were also more localized influences. For example, the anti-clerical Cathars, who had dualistic and Gnostic traits, possessed a great deal of influence in medieval Orvieto and surrounding rural areas. They were seen as heretics by the Catholic Church, which portrayed them collectively as the Antichrist. Second, we need to bear in mind that Signorelli was working at the turn of 1500, and there were a number of millennial (or half-millennial) fears, which included speculation about the Antichrist. For example, the Dominican priest Savonarola, active in nearby Florence, was executed in 1498 for heretical preaching about the end times. Third, some art historians have argued that these frescoes were specifically designed to fit in with the Church's Advent liturgy, of which the end times and Antichrist are a significant part. And finally, others have suggested that there could have been a significant communal drama at Orvieto in which the Antichrist figured as a character and that drew together some of these other strands, such as the demonization of Cathars and the Advent liturgy.

The rule of Antichrist

The portion of Signorelli's work that we're considering (see Figure 3.1) is probably the last of the frescoes to be finished and is the most complex. Bearing in mind that it was painted to be open to allegorical interpretation, how should we understand it? One entry point into this picture is via the pair of darkly dressed figures on the left. Some see these two characters as the artists – Fra Angelico and Signorelli. Others disagree and see a reference to God's 'two witnesses' at the Last Judgement mentioned in Revelation 11.3. Perhaps it is both. If we follow an arc above these two characters we see St Michael arriving in the sky, overcoming evil and as a sign of the end time. Below and to the right of St Michael we have the Antichrist on a plinth with the devil, giving him instructions, and behind them a group of clerics: four Dominicans, one canon and a Franciscan – who is pointing to St Michael.

A detailed inspection of the Antichrist and Satan shows how Signorelli has taken Fra Angelico's original painting of Christ but redrawn him with dissonant features. The Antichrist's facial features are akin but harder; the hair is a similar colour but wilder; the clothes are comparable colours but reversed. And, if we look closely, the figures of the Antichrist and the devil are intimately connected; they're so intertwined they're actually sharing arms.

Some have interpreted this image through mimetic theory as the rivalry of competitors, particularly brothers, which can be seen classically in the stories about Romulus and Remus, Oedipus and Creon, Cain and Abel, Richard the Lionheart and John Lackland, and we can recognize elements of this dynamic in the contemporary story of the two brothers Jamal and

Figure 3.1: Detail of Signorelli's fresco of The Rule of Antichrist *in the Cappella Nuova, Orvieto Cathedral, Italy. Image from the Web Gallery of Art and used with permission*

Salim in the Oscar-winning film *Slumdog Millionaire* (2008, dir. Danny Boyle). This picture shows a similar process being played out on a cosmic scale – Christ and Antichrist, God and Satan, the damned and the saved – as their rivalry and their conflict seek a resolution. And in the background we shouldn't forget the rivalries and conflicts of the time – the Cathars and the Church, the clerical holders of power and the anticlerical reformers.

Heaven and earth or leadership and management?

However, there is another way of viewing the binary between heaven and earth depicted in Signorelli's masterpiece. Sverre Spoelstra argues that the contemporary division between leadership and management is a mirror image of the theological division between heaven and earth. He sees contemporary notions of charismatic leadership as having their roots in notions of charisma from Christianity, which have been transferred into secular spheres by Nietzsche, Weber and others. Thus, he contends:

> leadership today is fundamentally considered against the background of a split between two spheres, the sphere of ordinary organization (business) and a higher sphere. The most familiar form that this split takes is the distinction between the manager, a function within the organization, and the leader, a person who transcends the organization and is therefore capable of doing something fundamental to it (e.g. 'transforming' it and infusing it with meaning). Leadership is seen as a force that transcends, redeems or complements 'ordinary' management and business. (Spoelstra, 2018, p. 43)

While such ideas were undoubtedly not in Signorelli's mind as he painted his *Last Judgement*, it is fascinating to bring them to his depiction of *The Rule of Antichrist*. On the earthly plane we have the organizational politics of everyday social and church life. This is emphasized by the figures of Antichrist and Satan raised above the crowd on a plinth and by the artist's depiction of the devil. As Sara Nair James has noted:

> Rather than follow tradition and depict the Devil as a gruesome composite beast of fantasy, Signorelli portrayed him as a life-size human, differentiated only by his nudity, scarlet horns and bat-like wings ... such a life-like image amplifies the insidiousness of the evil and duplicitous nature of Satan, who beguiles and can be indistinguishable from other human beings. (James, 2003, p. 69)

Dominating the background behind these two figures is Signorelli's image of Solomon's temple where, according to tradition, the Antichrist's throne is located and where his followers are killing the prophets Elijah and Enoch as they seek to take control.

Immediately behind the two figures seeking to wield authority from the plinth are a group of clergy engaged in earnest debate as they interpret various texts and Scriptures. Other sources of power are depicted in those clustered around Satan and Antichrist – styles of dress, wealth and bribes, force, conversation and argument. I would contend that the figures on the earthly plane are a study in followership, which we discussed in Chapter 2.3. The charismatic leadership is being provided by Satan (who is someone from beyond the 'ordinary' world) and is being mediated through the Antichrist. Spoelstra draws upon the work of the New Testament scholar Martin Hengel in identifying two forms of followership: 'to follow after' and 'to imitate' (Spoelstra, 2018, p. 106) and then engages with the theologian Dietrich Bonhoeffer to examine what following after means. There are two sides to this coin. First, following after can involve the leader presenting an extraordinary vision, which sets the direction of followers, and we have seen elements of this in our discussions of Jesus and his use of kingdom stories in previous chapters. Second, Spoelstra contends that Bonhoeffer believes following after Jesus implies that one is willing to break with established custom, traditions and authority (p. 107).

In terms of the other form of followership based upon imitation, Spoelstra says this is grounded on leading by example, where followers imitate the behaviour and values of their leader. His model here is that of kingship. This approach to following depends on stability:

> The king's sacredness is maintained by keeping him outside the normal order. In mythology, the king is often killed as soon as he appears to be human. The idea is that the centre of power, represented by the sacred king, must remain stable so that the kingdom, despite constant changes, also gains some stability. (p. 108)

We can see both forms of followership in Signorelli's fresco. In the foreground, gathered around Satan and Antichrist, are the imitators of their examples – taking bribes and seeking to exercise power. Behind them is the group of disparate clergy arguing over what is happening and what authority this new 'law' has. Further back is the temple, the seat of Antichrist's authority, and the soldiers seeking to bolster its social and cultural power.

How are these dynamics resolved in our contemporary world? Spoelstra states that when it comes to *charismatic* leadership there can only be one such leader and there is no space for others to manifest themselves in this role. If they do, they become a threat that has to be eliminated. Looking closely at Signorelli's work, we can see this is happening here too, as Satan is taking over and morphing into the figure of Antichrist. Eventually there will only be one charismatic leader – Satan.

Again, Spoelstra turns to Bonhoeffer, arguing that in the theologian's understanding of the call to follow after Jesus, 'Bonhoeffer ensures that the follower becomes part of a higher place without competition with Christ: the follower of Christ does not become Christ (does not take his place) but Christ lives within her' (Spoelstra, 2018, p. 112). We can see this too in Signorelli's painting of the sky, where there is a battle for control of the heavenly plane. The artist seeks to reassure viewers and worshippers that St Michael will vanquish the vain, earthly leadership of Satan that is seeking to take the place of Christ.

If we take Spoelstra's approach to leadership, then an engaged eschatology will seek to create meaning, particularly in situations where power is being abused and authority is being manipulated and misused. The kingdom stories told in such contexts will be crucial in this process of meaning-making, as James K. A. Smith says: 'Stories are like the air we breathe. Narrative is the scaffolding of our experience' (Smith, 2013, p. 108). Those stories can be told through multiple means – art, novels, biography, social media, organizational discourse, theology, to name just a few. We turn next to a site of more personal meaning-making and consider end of life and engaged eschatology.

3 End of life and engaged eschatology

'Death is nothing at all'

Henry Scott Holland was a canon of St Paul's Cathedral, London, from 1884 to 1910 and Regius Professor of Divinity, Oxford, from 1911 to 1918. Holland's most well-known theological work is his contribution on 'Faith' in *Lux Mundi* (Gore, 1890), but his thinking also had a significant impact upon such notable figures as the economic historian R. H. Tawney (Rowell, 2015) and the Archbishop of Canterbury, William Temple (Preston, 1983, p. 75). However, in contemporary culture he is most familiar for a reading that is very popular at funerals.

Any online search for 'poetry about death' or similar will provide multiple links to Holland's so-called poem 'Death is nothing at all', even though it is not a poem nor do the words quoted fully reflect his thinking about death. The oft-cited section reads:

Death is nothing at all. It does not count. I have only slipped away into the next room. Nothing has happened. Everything remains exactly as it was. I am I, and you are you, and the old life that we lived so fondly together is untouched, unchanged. Whatever we were to each other, that we are still. Call me by the old familiar name. Speak of me in the easy way which you always used. Put no difference into your tone. Wear no forced air of solemnity or sorrow. Laugh as we always laughed at the little jokes that we enjoyed together. Play, smile, think of me, pray for me. Let my name be ever the household word that it always was. Let it be spoken without an effort, without the ghost of a shadow upon it. Life means all that it ever meant. It is the same as it ever was. There is absolute and unbroken continuity. What is this death but a negligible accident? Why should I be out of mind because I am out of sight? I am but waiting for you, for an interval, somewhere very near, just round the corner. All is well.

This passage is part of Holland's sermon entitled 'Death the King of Terrors', preached at St Paul's in May 1910 following the death of King Edward VII.[1] In it, Holland contrasts 'two ways of regarding death, which appear to be in hopeless contradiction with each other'. The first he describes as an 'instinctive recoil from it as embodying the supreme and irrevocable disaster'. The second sees death as some kind of trick:

> It is not death; nobody is dead. It would be too ludicrous to suppose it. What has death to do with us? How can we die? Everything that we cared for and loved exists. Physical death has no meaning, no relation to it. Reason refuses to bring the two together.

This second perspective is given voice in the words about death being nothing at all, but Holland argues that these two views need to be reconciled, and spends the rest of his sermon seeking resolution.

Scott Holland at the movies

Before we see what form of resolution Holland achieved, I shall argue that we see the 'death is nothing at all' approach putting down significant roots in popular culture. Good examples of this are the films *The Shape of Water* (2017, dir. Guillermo del Toro) and *Coco* (2017, dir. Lee Unkrich).

The plot for *The Shape of Water* involves Elisa, who works at a government research centre where a hybrid fish–human discovered in South America is being kept, analysed and (in effect) tortured. By contrast, Elisa treats the creature well and eventually falls in love with it. The film's dialogue involves references to princes and princesses (kingdom) and to divinity (gods), but the movie's conclusion can be seen as providing an example of 'death is nothing at all' when the creature is trying to escape from its captors into its more natural habitat of the sea and takes Elisa there as well. This is not an environment in which she can survive, but the creature provides her with gills, so moving from land to water or from life to potential death through drowning is 'nothing at all'.

By contrast, *Coco* is explicitly about moving between the realms of the living and the dead. The film tells the story of Miguel, a young boy in Mexico who dreams of being a musician like his great hero Ernesto de la Cruz, whom he believes to be his great, great grandfather. However, for some reason music is banned in his household, so he escapes to enter a talent show on the Day of the Dead. The plot involves Miguel discovering family secrets and the truth about his great, great grandfather. For our purposes, the striking thing about this movie is the movement between the spheres of life and death. It is as if those who have died have not just 'slipped away into the next room' but slipped away into a neighbouring city and can be interacted with as long as certain conditions are met.

The question of which way influence is flowing can remain open. Thus, is the Scott Holland reading *contributing* to the broader cultural perceptions about death or is it popular because it is *reflecting* contemporary views? More pertinently, I would contend that Holland's resolution is a form of engaged eschatology. For Holland, the sense of being a child (or, in his terms, a 'son of God') is fundamental to faith and understanding the kingdom of heaven (Sachs, 1993, p. 153). As he goes on to say in that same sermon:

For we are already sons of God; already we are in Jesus; already we are of His Body; already we live by His life and taste His pardon and His peace. The Jesus whom we see and know now, is the Jesus whom we shall still see and know then; only, since we shall see Him nearer we shall grow more like Him; since we shall know Him better, we shall be more closely conformed to His image. Ah! why need we know more? Why should we be afraid of the great venture? We have Jesus now, and even now we can make ourselves more ready to draw closer to Him. We can begin to purify ourselves even as He is pure, to make ourselves more utterly His in the sure hope that at last we shall see Him as He is.

What sort of eschatology?

We might ask, is this a form of realized eschatology? That could be the case but, nevertheless, there remains a tension between the Jesus whom we see now and the one whom we shall see in the future. In other words, we are still living in that tension between the present and the future. Furthermore, Scott Holland's own thinking about these matters continued to develop, as David Nicholls has observed:

> Scott Holland, like many of his generation, was optimistic about human progress and he generally underestimated the power and persuasiveness of sin and evil. While it is only fair to say that, in his later writings, he recognised that the king-dom of heaven would not be realised on earth by a gradual development from within, but arrives from afar, his earlier work is characterised by a belief in the kingdom's 'gradual conquest of the world'. (Nicholls, 1989, p. 57)

I would argue that in Henry Scott Holland's popular reading as it is used for funerals we have but one side of an engaged eschatology. Within the context of death and bereavement we see that sense of God's future kingdom but without the corres-ponding sense of the present, including its painful separation or 'supreme and irrevocable disaster', in his words. There are kingdom stories that also illustrate this partial understanding, such as *The Shape of Water* and *Coco*, but we need to press on further in our conclusion to develop a fuller and more rounded eschatology of God's kingdom and its narrative implications.

Note

1 Read the whole sermon here: https://en.wikisource.org/wiki/The_King_of_Terrors (accessed 24.4.19).

4 The Church and kingdom stories: conclusion

Summary

As we have seen, Luca Signorelli is noted for his painting of the human body, and his frescoes in Orvieto's Cappella Nuova are a fine example of his craft. His depiction of the Last Judgement provides ample scope for portraying the human figure. In *The Rule of Antichrist* we see the heavenly and earthly planes of the narrative interacting as Satan seeks to exercise power in the earthly realm and to invade the heavenly sphere. There is a sense in which he is providing a vivid portrayal of an imminent eschatology, discussed in Chapter 1. The kingdom of God is physically breaking into space–time to end human history.

The recent ideas from Sverre Spoelstra discussed in this chapter helpfully illustrate the point David Sims and I have made in earlier works – *The Power of Story to Change a Church* (Roberts, 2017b, pp. 24–5) and *Leading by Story* (Roberts and Sims, 2017, pp. 188–91) – about the crucial need to listen to stories about the past and stories about the present. Spoelstra argues that this pattern of heavenly and earthly planes has transferred into business practice and organizational life. The divine economy (from the Greek word *oikonomia*, meaning 'household administration') has come to mean the management of our temporal realities. Stories from the past continue to influence stories told in the present.

He suggests that, given this heavenly origin of the term,

one may expect economic practices to be uncontaminated by the tactics and strategies that people use in everyday life to gain an advantage over others. But this is precisely not the case. The economy is a practice within the everyday life and partakes in human affairs by adopting some of the same means, including deception, condescension, punishment and lying. (Spoelstra, 2018, p. 131)

In other words, we see in our current social and organizational life precisely what Signorelli depicts under *The Rule of Antichrist*. Spoelstra contends that it is best to live with these tensions and paradoxes rather than seeking to escape them with, or without, a charismatic leader (p. 132). That approach seems to me to be a form of realized eschatology. How does engaged eschatology work in such circumstances?

If we seek to place the reading that Henry Scott Holland has (inadvertently) provided for many funerals on to Signorelli's masterpiece then that excerpt resides on the heavenly plane – even beyond the battle between Satan and St Michael, which we see in *The Rule of Antichrist*. However, as we have seen, Scott Holland's sermon also considers the earthly plane and the deep hurt and sorrow of grief. An equivalent to the turmoil and conflict of Signorelli's crowd scenes can be found in a fuller reading of that homily.

Bonhoeffer and eschatology

In his analysis of heaven and earth, Spoelstra draws upon the work of Dietrich Bonhoeffer, and we get another insight into the theological, organizational and artistic dynamics of this fresco from Sam Wells' analysis of Bonhoeffer's story and thinking. Wells describes three defining moments in the theologian's life. The first comes when he has left Germany for the United States in 1939 and is offered a post in New York that would have guaranteed his future security. However, he concludes:

> I have made a mistake in coming to America. I must live through this difficult period of our national history with the Christian people of Germany. I have no right to participate in the reconstruction of Christian life in Germany after the war if I do not share the trials of this time with my people. (quoted in Wells, 2015, p. 211)

The second defining moment for Bonhoeffer comes a year later, when he is sitting in a cafe in East Prussia at the time it was announced that France had surrendered. Everyone around him stood up and sang 'Deutschland über alles' and saluted Hitler. This brought a dawning realization that if the German people wanted Hitler gone they would have to do it themselves. The third and final defining moment comes in late 1944 when, after having been imprisoned, Bonhoeffer is planning to escape but realizes that to do so will place members of his close family in dire peril. The opportunity for freedom has passed, so Bonhoeffer remains incarcerated to meet whatever comes next with 'Christ's greatness of heart' (Wells, 2015, p. 218).

For Wells, Bonhoeffer's defining moments are summarized by these words from a passage written in prison and published in his *Ethics*:

> In Christ the reconciliation of the world with God took place. The world will be overcome not by destruction but by reconciliation. Not ideals or programs, not conscience, duty, responsibility, or virtue, but only the consummate love of God can meet and overcome reality. Again, this is accomplished not by a general idea of love, but by the love of God really lived in Jesus Christ. This love of God for the world does not withdraw from reality into noble souls detached from the world, but experiences and suffers the reality of the world at its worst. The world exhausts its rage on the body of Jesus Christ. But the martyred one forgives the world its sins. Thus reconciliation takes place. (p. 218)

On the face of it, there is little by way of reconciliation in Signorelli's work. The earthly plane is largely about battles for power – Satan exercising control through Antichrist, their followers through wealth and status, the quarrelling clergy through argument, soldiers through might. However, there are three pointers towards reconciliation. The first is in the death of the prophets, Enoch and Elijah, which could be an allusion to Jesus' lamentation over Jerusalem, the city of the Temple:

'Jerusalem, Jerusalem, the city that kills the prophets and stones those who are sent to it! How often have I desired to gather your children together as a hen gathers her brood under her wings, and you were not willing!' (Luke 13.34; see also Matthew 23.37). The second is that Signorelli has placed the fresco of *The Rule of Antichrist* above his depiction of Jesus' crucifixion, which is God's ultimate act of reconciliation or, to put it in Bonhoeffer's terms, an illustration of 'Christ's greatness of heart'. The third pointer is the liturgical context for the art, which for the most part reflects themes for All Saints and Advent. At some points, Signorelli also draws upon texts associated with Lent – notably Jesus' death and the resurrection of Lazarus (James, 2003, p. 79).

Wells' approach to Bonhoeffer also moves us beyond the binaries that we have focused on in this chapter – heaven and earth, leadership and management, death as 'nothing at all' or 'irrevocable disaster'. By placing eschatology within Bonhoeffer's life and personal story, we see how meaning is discovered and reconciliation between binaries of earth and heaven can be achieved, even the face of the irrevocable disaster of one's own impending death. The argument made throughout this book is that an engaged eschatology seeks to identify God's continued action in our world and in doing so resolves the binaries of imminent and realized eschatology by discerning, leading and telling contemporary kingdom stories inside and outside the Church. In the next chapter we shall explore how such an engaged eschatology can be discovered at work in the kingdom stories being told around contemporary acts of remembrance.

Prayer

Living God,
source of all wisdom and judgement,
in the cross of Jesus and the wonder of his empty tomb,
you lead us from death to life;
be with us in the depths of suffering
as you remained steadfast in Christ's crucifixion;
we ask this in the name of the One who came to save,
Jesus Christ our Lord. Amen.

On reflection

1 What significant works of art and popular culture engage you in a kingdom story?
2 Are there binary forms of thinking that shape your own meaning-making?
3 Where is Christ engaged in reconciliation in today's world?

4

One Kingdom Story in Detail

1 Introduction

In *So What's the Story ...?* (Glasson and Marsh, 2019), Barbara Glasson relates how she was involved in the Weaving Women's Wisdom project established by Touchstone, a Methodist interfaith initiative in the centre of Bradford, West Yorkshire. She describes how groups of women from different faith backgrounds were encouraged to meet and reflect on four questions:

- What is the wisest piece of advice I have been given?
- Who is/was the wisest woman in your life?
- Who are the wise women in your faith tradition?
- What is the difference between wisdom and knowledge?

Members of the group were supported as they engaged in conversation and designed rugs that reflected those conversations and their reactions to the exchanges.

In her observations about the project, Glasson notes:

Many of the rugs communicated deeply personal and painful stories. One group of women included asylum seekers who had recently arrived in the UK having fled Syria and North Africa. Although their English was fairly limited, the rug gave them the ability to tell their refugee stories. (Glasson and Marsh, 2019, p. 88)

Glasson was impressed by the rich depth of storytelling that enabled deeper levels of encounter between the participants of different faiths and cultures.

Some of the rugs placed those present-day stories into the narrative contexts of the various faiths within the group by referring directly to passages of Scriptures:

> One group compared the story of the Woman at the Well, in John's gospel and the pilgrimage of the Hajj made by many Muslims. The person of Hagar was discussed and the differences between the Hebrew Bible/Old Testament account and the Q'ran. This rug reflected the importance of water in holy narratives and also in everyday life, especially enabling the women to talk about times at which they shed tears. (Glasson and Marsh, 2019, p. 89)[1]

Such use of a material project that allows people to express aspects of their personal and communal stories is not uncommon. This chapter will explore in depth an undertaking by one church to commemorate the one hundredth anniversary of the end of the First World War and the kinds of narrative that were woven into this venture. I shall begin by outlining the background story and the outcomes from the project before examining some of the other forms of narrative that reflect on what transpired. Once again, I would contend that this is a form of engaged eschatology that makes connections with different kinds of kingdom story.

Note

1 The longstanding connection in Britain between sheep farming and the woollen industry with abbeys and monasticism is noted by Esther Rutter (2019, pp. 105–6).

2 What was the story?

Warwick Poppies was a project in 2018 to mark the centenary anniversary of the end of the First World War in St Mary's Church, Warwick. This is a large civic church in the centre of a county town in the English Midlands. Warwick is probably best known for Warwick Castle, originally the ancestral home of the Beauchamp family, who arrived in the country with William the Conqueror. However, in more recent times the castle has been owned by Merlin Entertainments and run as a tourist attraction.

According to David Brindley:

> The Beauchamps were perhaps the most consistently successful family among the English nobility for a period approaching two centuries. They acquired the title of earl of Warwick by good fortune rather than by judgement, and managed to hang on to it by producing a male heir who grew into adulthood in each generation – an achievement equalled by few other aristocratic families in an age when infant mortality was high. (Brindley, 2001, p. 10)

The Lady Chapel established by the Beauchamp dynasty in the fifteenth century marks the last resting place of various family members; there is also a family vault in the crypt, situated in the church's Norman foundations. It was originally built by Richard Beauchamp, reputedly the richest person in the kingdom and the model for Chaucer's knight in his *Canterbury Tales*, as his final resting place.

Furthermore, Brindley notes that there was almost no military campaign in the closing centuries of the Middle Ages in which an Earl of Warwick did not play a major role. This military connection with the church has continued into the present day with the presence of the Regimental Chapel for the Royal Warwickshire Regiment, which played a significant part in the Great War, as it was sometimes known.

Each year as Christmas approaches, St Mary's holds a

Figure 4.1: Women's Institute Christmas tree 2016 (photograph by Veronica Chapman)

Christmas-tree festival in the church, where local businesses, schools, voluntary organizations and charities are invited to dress a tree. Visitors to the church are then invited to choose their favourite. In 2016 the Women's Institute decorated their tree with knitted poppies and was voted the winner (see Figure 4.1). From this, an idea was conceived to invite people to knit poppies for the Regimental Chapel as a way of commemorating the 2018 anniversary. The plan was to get 11,610 poppies – one for each of the fallen from the regiment. The project was launched in church on 5 September 2017.[1] The quantitative outcomes from the project were striking and greatly exceeded the expectations of the organizers.

Note

1 The launch video can be found here: www.youtube.com/watch?v=zym_GxO2vMk (accessed 21.5.19).

3 What were the outcomes?

Figure 4.2: Some of the 65,000 poppies displayed in St Mary's Church during the exhibition (photograph by Gillian Fletcher)

Outcomes from the Warwick Poppies project were striking. The number of poppies collected was over 65,000 (see Figure 4.2), including contributions from the USA, Canada, Brazil, France, Holland, Belgium, Australia, New Zealand, India, South Africa and wider continental Africa, Russia and Greenland. St Mary's annual visitor numbers are around 37,000, yet in the project's three-month period they were 47,000. The total number of people attending services on Remembrance Sunday is usually around 600. Attendance on that Sunday in 2018 was 1,490 (plus another 500 for a special weekday service arranged for local schools). The weekly turnover in the church shop increased by around a factor of ten and included visitors who wanted to buy a knitted poppy as a memento. The prayers written to accompany the display proved so popular that they were made into a booklet for people to take away.

4 Why did this happen?

There are some easily identifiable reasons at a national level that explain why this happened: (i) 2018 was the centenary of the end of the First World War and there was considerable national interest in marking this anniversary, as well as other similar projects that caught community enthusiasm; (ii) in the UK there has been a steady rise in numbers attending religious services and acts of remembrance on Remembrance Sunday and Armistice Day following the Falklands conflict (1982) and British military involvement in Afghanistan (from 2001) and Iraq (from 2003); (iii) the National Curriculum for England was introduced by the Education Reform Act of 1988, which brought the study of the Second World War into the history syllabus; (iv) the *Blood Swept Lands and Seas of Red* display of red ceramic poppies at the Tower of London in 2014, designed by Tom Piper and created by Paul Cummins, commemorating the start of the First World War, created a desire for larger-scale poppy displays.

At a more local level, the interest in local media, where it was featured on BBC and ITV regional news broadcasts as well as local radio, generated a great deal of interest. In addition, the organizers used social media to engage with individuals and communities of interest. However, I shall argue that a kingdom story approach to the Warwick Poppies narrative can identify significant changes in how some individuals and communities are telling and sharing their stories in contemporary society.

5 What are the implications for ministry and story?

I want to explore more deeply what the potential implications are for a storytelling and story-sharing approach to ministry and leadership. This qualitative analysis of the Warwick Poppies project will identify six narrative strands that have implications for a storied approach to leading churches:

  i stories online
 ii 'control' of stories
iii structuring of people's life stories
 iv seeking transcendent (bigger) stories
  v ending stories
 vi losing stories.

(i) Importance of social media – stories online

The use of traditional media in spreading the news about events such as Warwick Poppies remains an important part of this narrative. Local news channels on the BBC and ITV networks carried lengthy reports about the display (BBC *Midlands Today* recorded and broadcast in late October 2018 and *ITV News Central* recorded and broadcast in early November 2018). Local newspapers also publicized the story. Not surprisingly perhaps, the *Warwick Courier* ran stories that marked the opening of the display,[1] its ongoing success,[2] its impact in fund-raising for the Royal British Legion and St Mary's Church,[3] the opportunity to buy your own knitted poppy after the project had finished,[4] and the project's community award from the High Sheriff of Warwickshire.[5]

In addition to the established television and print media, Warwick Poppies also made extensive use of social media, particularly Facebook and Twitter.[6] With this approach the project reflected something of the changing nature of observing and ritualizing death in twenty-first-century Western cultures. In her research into how people's online existence is changing the landscape of death and grief, Debra Bassett observes:

The need to look at people as having lived and having a narrative rather than just becoming 'the deceased' was once the job of the clergy, obituary writers and eulogy writers. Respect for the dead requires remembering the dead. The need to be remembered and the ability to pass on memories is an ancient need: from the first cave drawings and the magnificent mausoleums of the Egyptians, we can see that symbols of man's quest for immortality are well chronicled. (Bassett, 2015, p. 1134)

Yet as Bassett goes on to point out, people's online existence means that it is now possible for everyone to start creating their own digital 'mausoleum', not just pharaohs, monarchs and those with power: 'through recent communication technology, it is now possible for "ordinary" people to create and curate their own narratives, ensuring that they leave behind digital memories for others' (p. 1135).

The role of social media in bereavement is not confined to imitating the means of past memorializing as it is also providing new challenges. Those who have died are 'leaking into everyday life' as they continue to be 'popping up on social media sites' (Bassett, 2018a, npn). It is estimated that 8,000 Facebook members die daily and their digital afterlives are affecting how people grieve for them. One of the ways in which the nature of grief is changing is the rise of concern over 'second death' or 'second loss', resulting from technical obsolescence of hardware and a loss of digital data and the narrative of a loved one's life. There are companies that are seeking to create spaces to store individuals' life experiences and stories (Bassett, 2018b).

The impact of social media is not just about the online present and the potential digital future. The relative ease with which people can now research their ancestors online means that there is a greater awareness of how many forebears may have been involved in past conflicts, such as the First World War. In the UK these digital changes and increase in familial information have coincided with changes to education.

The introduction of the National Curriculum for England in 1988 and teaching about the Second World War has raised the level of awareness about more recent conflicts and their role in forming contemporary British life, culture and story.

The Warwick Poppies project is a kingdom story in many ways but not least because it is about people making sense of their personal narratives, the stories of their families and how those stories fit into the story of British, European and world history. At the level of a communal story this is illustrated by 250 people gathering by the Warwick Town war memorial at 6.30 a.m. to hear a lone piper play the same tune that was played 100 years earlier at the conclusion of the Second World War and then enter church to hear more tunes, including 'Amazing Grace'. By contrast, at the level of a single family, while the display was running, a circus visited Warwick and a couple came to commemorate a great uncle who was a performer at that same circus and who also served in the Great War. An engaged eschatology that is alive to kingdom stories can make those important connections.

(ii) The role of nostalgia in early twenty-first-century UK – 'control' of stories

In previous chapters we have touched on the role of power in kingdom stories and we see that again in the role that nostalgia plays in society. In a piece published in 1993 and more recently made available on his website, Yiannis Gabriel stated:

> The study of nostalgia has grown in recent years, as nostalgia itself has assumed a dominant place in Western cultures. Whole sectors of the economy are fuelled by nostalgia. The heritage and tourist industries, a large section of entertainment, music and the arts continuously strive to feed people's yearning for a golden past. In the hands of advertisers, nostalgia has become a tried and tested if over-used device for promoting anything from potato crisps to insurance policies.

The film industry has become dominated by endless recycling of themes and archetypes from the past, full of references to classic movies and sequels to not-so-classic ones which then come to be seen as classic. Television forever repeats its own golden oldies. Politicians, like Thatcher and Reagan, built substantial support by mobilizing nostalgia for an earlier era, a mythologised past of authentic values and heroic achievements. (Gabriel, 1993)

It is easy to see the patterns he is describing being repeated in contemporary culture. Nostalgia is very powerful and visible nearly 30 years later in such slogans and movements as 'Take Back Control' (Brexit), 'Make America Great Again' (MAGA) and the rise in political populism in a number of Western cultures. Nostalgia provides an anchor at a time of great change, and it was notable that the final editorial in *The Economist* for the year of the Warwick Poppies commemoration was on nostalgia: 'When nothing seems to make sense, history becomes the supreme discipline. Knowing who you are and where you come from matters' ('The uses of nostalgia', leader in *The Economist*, 22 December 2018, p. 11).

In his discussion of organizational nostalgia, Gabriel identified three key elements: buildings, leaders, and other characters and departed colleagues. We can see some of those elements in the story of Warwick Poppies: the significance of both St Mary's Church and the town's war memorial as places that help to structure memory and tell stories; the importance of having community leaders involved – the Bishop of Warwick was at the launch event and the 2018 Remembrance Sunday service; and departed family and friends were the ever-present focus of the display. Having said that, Gabriel concludes:

organizational nostalgia tells us more about the discontents of today than about the contents of yester-year. Like humour, but in a radically different way, it seeks to provide a symbolic way out of the rigours of bureaucracy, seeking to re-enchant a long disenchanted world. Having lost faith in the future, it idealizes the past, constructing an ego-ideal out of what has been rather than about what should become. (Gabriel, 1993).

A simple story that illustrates Gabriel's point is that while Warwick Poppies was taking place, the UK was continuing its negotiations about leaving the European Union. One Wednesday morning a regular attender at the midweek Holy Communion service came out of the Regimental Chapel into the nave, which was awash with poppies, and said to me, 'If only our enemies in Brussels could see this.' The irony was that two of the leading lights (if not *the* leading lights) behind the display were very strongly in favour of remaining in the EU. That is just one small example of a discontent from one era being projected back on to nostalgia for the past.

Significantly, Margaret MacMillan, in her book on the 1919 Paris Conference and its attempt to 'end' the Great War, finishes by stating:

> The peacemakers, however, had to deal with reality, not what might have been. They grappled with huge and difficult questions. How can irrational passions of nationalism or religion be contained before they do more damage? How could we outlaw war? We are still asking those questions (MacMillan, 2001, p. 500)

I would argue that a better way of seeing those dynamics, rather than as merely 'irrational passions', is to understand them as competing narratives that the storytellers seek to use to establish authority and power. We saw in the previous chapter, with the discrete analyses of Bonhoeffer's theology by Sverre Spoelstra and Samuel Wells, how Jesus' use of kingdom stories in first-century Palestine and Bonhoeffer's use of kingdom stories in twentieth-century Germany were all part of a deeper narrative pool with many competing eddies, currents and vortices.[7]

(iii) Structuring of people's life stories

Catholic and Orthodox Christians have long appreciated the value of ritual in liturgy and life, and evangelical Christians appear to be rediscovering it as well. Good examples are the work of James K. A. Smith and A. Scott Moreau. Smith contends that all communal rituals are a form of 'liturgy' that can take on Christian and secular forms. He believes that 'To say we are liturgical animals is simultaneously to emphasise that we are metaphorical animals, imaginative animals, poetic animals, "storied" animals' (Smith, 2013, pp. 126–7). Alongside this approach, Moreau recounts how he grew up experiencing ritual as 'boring, meaningless and empty', but his children have developed a very different vantage point:

> As they grew up they began to seek out churches that practice the very rituals I wanted to avoid. They explained to me that they want to participate in something that has centuries-long roots rather than something that was developed over the past few decades. (Moreau, 2018, p. 162)

He thinks that within contemporary Western societies this is not uncommon.

One expression of this development can be found in a return to a way of life structured by special days. During pre-Reformation times it was saints' days but now this human need finds expression in events like Alzheimer's Awareness Day, World Diabetes Day, Buy Your Priest a Beer Day. There are times when the older, sacred order and newer, secular order come together, and Remembrance is one of those. In his discussion about the nature of time, George Guiver notes how there are special times for special things, such as April Fool's Day when pranks are legitimized. He describes how for some cultures at Christmas there is

> an especially powerful interruption of the eternal into time. We do not simply hear the same old story again. It becomes

real. On that night Mary and Joseph *are* in the stable and the baby *is* in the manager. It is as if they are always there in an eternal time, and once a year we drop into it. (Guiver, 1988, p. 14 – emphasis original)

Guiver goes on to illustrate this further by quoting a letter written by an army officer killed in the First World War who drew attention to the fact that life and time are both about quality rather than quantity.[8] Rituals or, to use Smith's term, 'cultural liturgies', help individuals and societies to structure their times and seasons. I am not saying that Buy Your Priest a Beer Day is of the same significance as Remembrance Sunday – clearly that is not the case. However, they are both a part of the same process of ordering time and providing structure for people's life stories.

In addition to the importance of time, Moreau identifies five crucial functions that ritual serves: (a) establishing and maintaining individual and group identity; (b) generating new order to prevent individuals and societies from falling apart; (c) enabling social transition; (d) functioning as symbolic repositories for cultural values and traditions; (e) enabling people to experience the transcendent and connect with those spirits, ancestors and gods in which they believe. We can see a number of these elements in the rituals of remembrance linked to poppies and the commemoration of those who have fallen in wars and conflict. Knitting has numerous connections to this sense of order and structure.

Esther Rutter describes the role of knitted scarves in the culture of soccer, which includes a photograph from the 1950s of five supporters heading to see their football team playing in an FA Cup semi-final. One of the blue and white scarves is embroidered with the names of the team, and Rutter describes this as 'a once-sacred litany of players' (2019, p. 281). She continues: 'More than simply a statement of support, this scarf plots history … It is their blue and white miniature Bayeux' (p. 281). There is a sense in which the Warwick Poppies project is another expression of the knitted ordering of human lives.

One of the things that surprised organizers of Warwick Poppies was the desire of people to take home a memento of their visit. Many came into the church shop asking to buy one of the knitted poppies, so a basket of them was put out for visitors to make purchases. It is highly probable that a number of different factors were in play here, both consciously and sub-consciously. In terms of Moreau's functions of ritual it is likely that a sense of identity is being established (a) and the flowers themselves were functioning as symbolic repositories for cultural values (b). It is also possible that they enabled some social transition (c) of moving from a place of remembrance (the church) back into the world (the high street). I would contend that for many they also helped to connect their stories with those of their 'ancestors and gods' (e).

We can see in the number of visitors to Warwick Poppies how some of the ritualized behaviour associated with ancient rituals of 'pilgrimage' continues to have spiritual power and connection, which is another way in which this story also functions as a kingdom story. We can see this too in the popularity of a series of programmes at Easter time about various celebrities making pilgrimages to Santiago de Compostela and Rome,[9] and with Simon Reeve's series of documentaries about pilgrimage to Canterbury, Rome and Jerusalem.

(iv) The place of religion in the early twenty-first-century UK – seeking bigger stories

Atul Gawande is a surgeon and professor at Harvard Medical School who has explored changing perceptions and experiences of death in his book *Being Mortal* (Gawande, 2014). He points out how surviving into old age was comparatively rare in the past but longevity is now much more common in many societies. Elders were once seen as repositories of knowledge and wisdom but less so now. Certainly if we have a question about technology we ask a search engine or a teenager. And for many, the traditional family system has become, 'less a source of security than a struggle for control – over property, finance, and even the most basic decisions about how they live' (Gawande, 2014, p. 19).

As he explores the various changes he draws upon the work of the philosopher Josiah Royce, set out in his book *The Philosophy of Loyalty* (1908), which addressed the question of why simply existing seems empty and meaningless to people. Royce's answer was that

> we all seek a cause beyond ourselves. This was, to him, an intrinsic human need. The cause could be large (family, country, principle) or small (a building project, the care of a pet). The important thing was that, in ascribing value to the cause and seeing it as worth making sacrifices for, we give our lives meaning. (Gawande, 2014, p. 126)

Thus, Gawande argues, the only way to overcome the meaninglessness of death is to see oneself as part of something greater, and, as life extends, those things that give meaning tend to be less about achievements and accumulation and more about life's simpler pleasures.

He puts this in narrative terms when he says that as people become more aware of the finitude of their life:

> All we ask is to be allowed to remain writers of our own story. That story is ever changing. Over the course of our lives, we may encounter unimaginable difficulties. Our concerns and desires may shift. But whatever happens, we want to retain the freedom to shape our lives in ways consistent with our character and loyalties. (pp. 140–1)

Significantly, he returns to the analogy of story-writing towards the end of his book, when he notes: 'For human beings, life is meaningful because it is a story. A story has a sense of a whole, and its arc is determined by the significant moments, the ones where something happens' (p. 238). And a crucial element in this is that, 'in stories, endings matter' (p. 239).

Similar themes have been developed from the perspective of Christian theology in the work of Sam Wells. He argues that being with those who are dying comes in two kinds:

> There's being with those who recognise, as best they can, what's in prospect, have taken stock of what can and cannot be done, and are resolved to use aright the time that is left to them on earth; and there are those who are trying as hard as they can not to name or entertain what lies ahead. (Wells, 2017, p. 202)

Yet he also admits that these two approaches to death are not utterly distinct and that there can be 'traffic between them' (p. 202). The implication is that there are those who are seeking a meaningful ending to their stories and there are those who are not (yet) able to contemplate a conclusion to their personal narrative. This can have profound implications not just for those who are dying but also for those who are waiting and watching alongside, because the dying and those with them 'experience a deeper dimension of living than those who are not dying' (p. 203).

In his discussion of being with those who have forms of dementia, John Swinton talks about the difference between 'clock time' and 'providential time'. There is an important eschatological element here, which provides time with a sense of meaning. In other words:

> Time is not empty. Each moment is filled with meaning, new possibilities, and eschatological hope. If time is meaningful, then taking time to be with a person with severe dementia is meaningful, purposeful, and revelatory even if it may not always feel that way at the time. If time is meaningful, we should look for the meaning in each of our encounters. (Swinton, 2012, p. 235)

These encounters will be storied encounters – encompass-
ing narratives past and present, which also contribute to the
stories of the future. And the same is true about the experience
of being with those who are dying. In terms of this interaction
between one's own story and the bigger reality of death, Wells
notes that 'There's no objective estimation of what's taking
place: there's only the dying person's narrative, and such com-
plementary or counternarratives offered by those around them'
(Wells, 2017, p. 205).[10]

The stories collected by Kathryn Mannix, a consultant in
palliative care, in her book *With the End in Mind* (2017), illustrate how human beings continue to seek transcendence (or
'bigger' stories) in many different forms, and times of shared
remembrance can bring all these together. Her final section is
entitled 'Transcendence' and, like Gawande, she notes how
important frameworks of value and purpose are for people's
lives. Some of these will be religious or political, others based
in nature or the vast unfolding of the universe, and yet others
find them in music, art or poetry. Significantly, the end of life
can be a time when many people make a 'spiritual reckoning'
of their worth and the meaning of life that is ebbing:

> they seek to transcend the difficulties that beset them, and to
> consider a bigger picture. This impulse allows extraordinary
> acts of courage and devotion, of humility and compassion,
> supported and validated by their personal spiritual con-
> structs. It is perhaps that spiritual dimension of humanness
> that reveals us at our very best, even (or perhaps especially)
> here at the edge of life. (Mannix, 2017, pp. 275–6)

Remembrance Sunday, Armistice Day, Warwick Poppies 2018
and other knitted poppy projects are about all of these things.
They tap into people's quest for meaning in their lives and the
role that large- and small-scale causes, such as country and
family, can play in that search. This pursuit of meaning was
reflected in such comments as 'I'm not religious but this feels
really spiritual' and 'I'm not Christian but I lead a Christian

life'. By coming to view the display or by knitting a poppy, people felt part of something bigger and were aware that there was a shared sense of meaning-making taking place, even if it was also individual and potentially unformed or inchoate. I would contend that it also connected with the current interest in mindfulness. If they wished, people could walk around the church with their own thoughts and make connections with their inner lives. In the words of Moreau, they could connect their stories with those of their 'ancestors and gods' as part of a generalized seeking after transcendence and meaning.[11] The project was also about the endings of stories, which we turn to next.

(v) Approaches to death in the early twenty-first-century UK – ending stories

In February 2018 I took a funeral for Scott 'Boz' Bosley, who was 29 and had been tragically stabbed to death after watching Aston Villa, the team he supported, playing on television in a local pub. I have deliberately not anonymized him because Scott was a real person with his own story. And his story intertwined with mine in a number of ways. We supported the same soccer team; when I went dog-walking we often travelled along the road on which Scott lived, and the pub in which he was watching the match and the spot where he was very sadly killed were near to where the Warwick Team churches ran a coffee shop.

Although his funeral was held in a traditional church building, it was far from traditional in itself. There were no hymns; instead, the music was 'Hey Brother' and 'The Nights' by Avicii,[12] and 'Skin' by Rag'n'Bone Man.[13] The readings were two popular poems – 'The Dash' by Linda Ellis (which has its own official website[14]) and 'Do not Stand at my Grave and Weep' by Mary Elizabeth Frye.[15] His family and friends were encouraged to attend wearing the colours of his football team, so the church was a sea of claret and blue.

The way in which Boz's family chose to mark his death is not unusual in Western culture. A report for the *Washington Post* in April 2019 highlights the changing nature of how death is ritualized:

> many families are replacing funerals (during which the body is present) with memorial services (during which the body is not). Religious burial requirements are less a consideration in a country where 36% of Americans say they regularly attend religious services, nearly a third never or rarely attend and almost a quarter identify as agnostic or atheist, according to the Pew Research Center.

Grief was undoubtedly a significant aspect of Boz's funeral but, according to the *Washington Post*:

> Some practitioners worry that death has taken a holiday, and grief is too frequently banished in end-of-life celebrations that seem like birthday blowouts. 'Do you think we're getting too happy with this?' asks Amy Cunningham, director of *The Inspired Funeral* in Brooklyn. 'You can't pay tribute to someone who has died without acknowledging the death and sadness around it. You still have to dip into reality and not ignore the fact that they're absent now.'[16]

The use of different forms of popular culture in funerals, memorials and thanksgivings illustrates the fluid nature of bereavement in various contemporary societies. It could be argued that Warwick Poppies is another manifestation of this since knitting is another mode of popular culture. However, I would argue that a project like this brings together newer and more traditional approaches to grief ritual.

As part of the Warwick Poppies project, Kirsteen Robson, a member of St Mary's Church and writer of the monthly church prayer diary, co-ordinated a team to create a series of 20 prayers for visitors, which were placed around the poppy display. The prayers proved so popular that people wanted to take them away. They were collected into a booklet entitled *A Time to Remember*, which visitors could purchase for a nominal sum to cover the printing costs. The title was drawn from a well-known passage in Ecclesiastes 3, which was printed inside the front cover:

A Time for Everything

There is a time for everything,
and a season for every activity under the heavens:
a time to be born and a time to die,
a time to plant and a time to uproot,
a time to kill and a time to heal,
a time to tear down and a time to build,
a time to weep and a time to laugh,
a time to mourn and a time to dance,
a time to scatter stones and a time to gather them,
a time to embrace and a time to refrain from embracing,
a time to search and a time to give up,
a time to keep and a time to throw away,
a time to tear and a time to mend,
a time to be silent and a time to speak,
a time to love and a time to hate,
a time for war and a time for peace.
(Ecclesiastes 3.1–8, NIV)

In his discussion of Ecclesiastes and this passage in particular, John Barton argues that the book is concerned with finding meaning in life and denies such a thing can be found. He points out that the final line from this passage – 'What gain have the workers from their toil?' – is often omitted, as in the case of the Warwick Poppies prayer booklet. In essence he believes that Ecclesiastes is 'in effect a parody of a wisdom book, undermining the whole wisdom enterprise' (Barton, 2019, p. 68). Having said that, he goes on to describe the role of wisdom literature as inviting 'the reader into a dialogue about human life and its patterns, rather than laying down the law'. It tends to be open-ended rather than dogmatic: 'if it offers insight into the world and its ways, it is by proposing proverbs and wise sayings to ponder, not rigid diktats to be accepted and adhered to' (p. 69). This open-ended approach was at the heart of the Warwick Poppies exhibition and the prayer trail. It offered some traditional ways of finding meaning in the experience of viewing the poppy display but did not impose it. In other words, it was an invitation into shared dialogue, meaning-making and storytelling.

According to Kirsteen Robson, the idea for the prayer trail sprang from an email from a member of the congregation,

> asking if a prayer could be made available at the back of church, as she knew of a couple of people who had visited the Poppies on the first day and had been, in her words, 'a bit distressed and in need of a hug'. This included a gentleman who had served in the Second World War and his father had been in the First World War and so he was remembering both wars. The realization then hit me that we were inviting people into this highly moving and potentially overwhelming display, and that we should be offering some emotional and spiritual support. Somehow it didn't feel as though one prayer would be enough, and then I suddenly saw the whole display as an invitation for people to reflect and talk to God, and things went from there.

The prayers were written for people of any faith or none, of many nationalities and backgrounds, and many different circumstances. They may have lost relatives in the world wars or more recent conflicts, be families of people in active service, relations of conscientious objectors, politicians and more. So while they were written to be as open as possible, they also reflected the formal structure of liturgical prayers found in many churches. Here is one good example:

God of healing ...

We remember the victims of humanity's inhumanity; survivors scarred in body or mind through the ravages of war. We pray for those whose injuries denied or still deny them the life once enjoyed. We pray for those who bore or still bear their mental anguish in silence, unable to voice their suffering. We remember too the families who cared or still care for those in pain, facing a future forever changed. May all who suffered rest in your healing arms for eternity. May all who still suffer be surrounded with your love and healing presence, knowing that, whatever happens, you will never forsake them. Lest we forget. Amen.

And be sure of this: I am with you always, even to the end of the age.

(Matthew 28.20)

Bereavement is an intensely personal experience as people grieve in different ways and need to find appropriate endings to individual stories. In a similar way to how the more formal prayers for Warwick Poppies left space open for people to bring their own beliefs to the prayer trail, so within Boz Bosley's funeral there was also space for statements of faith. For instance, in his eulogy Boz's father wrote: 'It all started on the 18th June 1988 when he was born. I picked him up and cried my eyes out, over the joy of God for giving me my son.' And he concluded: 'Now he has been taken away from me, I'll never forget him, my heart is so full of love for him and I know *I really believe that we shall meet again one day and I cannot wait for that day to come around*' (italics in the original). This reflects some of the narrative and openness that was described at the conclusion of Chapter 2.

We can see another instance of this need to be open at the close of stories in popular culture as well. The BBC TV series *Blackadder Goes Forth* (1989, dir. Richard Boden) concludes with a number of storied moments involving the central characters. First, Captain Darling outlines his nostalgic hopes for his life were he to survive the war. His personal narrative would be structured by marriage, job and cricket. The main characters then join the other troops in the trenches to await the signal for going over the top. The guns fall silent and they speculate about what is happening in the bigger story – 'Maybe the war's over?' 'The big knobs have got around the table and yanked the iron out of the fire!' 'Thank God, we lived through it – the Great War 1914 to 1917 ...' But it is clear that is not the case. The ending of the story and the end of the *Blackadder* comedy series is a scene of pathos as the soldiers run into enemy fire and the image of conflict fades into a field of poppies with the show's theme tune being played at a funereal pace.[17] As funerals become a celebration of people's lives, what happens to our genuine feelings of sorrow, sadness and grief? Remembrance is a rare time to recall solemnly those who have died.

(vi) Memory loss – losing stories

At the conclusion to Chapter 3 we discussed the eschatological tension between living in the present and living in the future, and how Bonhoeffer's theology encourages us to move beyond seeing the world, our experience and God's kingdom in terms of simple binaries. In his book *Dementia*, John Swinton begins with Bonhoeffer's answer to the question, 'Who am I?' The response that Swinton finds in Bonhoeffer's work is: 'In the end only God knows who we are; only God can search our hearts and recognize who we really are. God creates us, sustains us, and knows us' (Swinton, 2012. p. 5). In this process of knowing and being known, Swinton ascribes a vital role for human beings as storytelling creatures and contends that the diversity of stories we tell comes 'together to give us a sense of who we are and where we are located within the ongoing stories of our lives' (p. 22). As more and more people experience dementia within their own lives through memory loss in parents, spouses, partners, friends and others, one of the other needs that collective acts of remembrance can provide for is an acknowledgement of how important memory is and that when it dies that, in itself, can be a huge bereavement – even if the embodied person continues to live on. I'd argue that consciously or subconsciously there are people actively bringing that grief to Remembrance commemorations as well.

Having said that, Swinton, reflecting on the work of Stanley Hauerwas, also argues: 'We are not the authors of our own stories. Our calling is to learn how to read and interpret the story of God faithfully and well. In this sense people with dementia are reminded and remind us of this fundamental fact about the world' (p. 164). I would contend that in terms of kingdom stories this is a false binary and that it is perfectly possible to read and interpret the story of God faithfully and well while at the same time being the authors of our own stories. In fact, I would go further and say that the writing of individual and shared kingdom stories is the bringing together of God's story and our stories.

Sam Wells has also drawn upon a story about dementia to illustrate how he understands the kingdom of God.[18] He tells of a congregation member at St Martin-in-the-Fields who attended two evenings organized around dementia and faith, and then on the third evening with the help of two friends told the story of her life and her own experience of Alzheimer's. Wells saw this in terms of the account of people bringing their friend to Jesus on a stretcher for healing:

in that moment I saw what prophetic ministry means. Not berating authorities, not denouncing congregations, not excoriating government; but slowly, patiently, building sufficient trust with a person who is socially excluded, not assuming that one has to speak on their behalf, but over a transformative meal, listening, taking notes, assembling thoughts, so that one day, with a fair wind and a sympathetic audience, that person could speak her own words, sing her true song, and let the whole room thud with the sound of jaws dropping. (Wells, 2019, npn)

This is a good example of a kingdom story and the transformative power of engaged eschatology.

Of course the profound challenges of dementia and Alzheimer's go much deeper, as Swinton makes clear. A key element here is our varied notions of personhood. Swinton begins by drawing upon John Locke's definition of a person rooted in human beings as conscious, thinking creatures, and therefore 'defined in terms of capacity for self-awareness, identity, continuity of thinking, a sense of self over time, conscious, and above all memory' (Swinton, 2012, p. 123). This can result in the paradox that some people are left in the final years of their lives as 'non-persons' or people who seem to have to some extent effectively vanished. However, in Swinton's terms personal memory is not just about self. Some of it is held by the individual, but some is also held by others, and all of it is held by God – a good proportion of our memories are retained and retold outside of ourselves: 'when some things are far from clear in our own minds, we are able to experience a sense of self through the memories of us held by those around us, through the stories they tell about us. Memory, like mind and personhood, is corporate through and through' (p. 221).

My contention is that while commemorations such as Remembrance Sunday and Armistice Day, together with anniversaries marking the beginning and end of significant conflicts (represented by displays such as Warwick Poppies 2018), are undoubtedly memorializing those who have died and been injured in war, they are also providing space for people to process the many different forms of grief found in contemporary society, including grieving the loss of a loved one's memory even though she or he remains bodily alive. For both Wells and Swinton, the importance of being with individuals and communities is crucial.

6 One kingdom story in detail: conclusion

This chapter has used a narrative approach to analyse the Warwick Poppies commemoration of the one hundredth anniversary of the conclusion of the First World War. It has identified six specific areas where stories have been important: (i) stories online; (ii) 'control' of stories; (iii) structuring of people's life stories; (iv) seeking bigger stories; (v) ending stories; (vi) losing stories. In *Leading by Story* (2017), David Sims and I mapped out a series of nine improvised stories that shape ministry in local churches and that clergy and others will find themselves leading. These are the improvised narratives around finance, architecture, governance, pastoral care, mission, education, media, art and unintended stories.

There is a sense in which the Warwick Poppies project is one extended unintended story. At the outset there was no certainty that the original target of 11,610 poppies could be met, and the fact that there was such a response in terms of knitted poppies donated and visitor numbers meant that the project was, in a sense, one long narrative of improvisation. The six stories identified in this account of the project connect to some of the narratives outlined and previously discussed. For instance, stories about pastoral care, mission, education, media and art are clearly part of this account. However, there are also untold stories about how the project was financed and the impact it had upon the church's architecture, which may be for another occasion.

In terms of the ideas about kingdom stories discussed in this book, I would argue that the Warwick Poppies project is a good example of engaged eschatology, or the process of seeking for signs of God's kingdom in the world around us and in people's daily lives. In addition to the stories already discussed, another simple example is that the venture also benefited from local supermarket staff spending some of their volunteer time on it and engaging with the church. Something of this eschatological understanding is expressed, it seems to me, in Sam Wells' 2019 Inclusive Church annual lecture, in which he discusses heaven and the kingdom of God. Although he begins by considering these as things that lie in the future, he also considers their present implications, stating:

> Our way to *live* eschatologically is not to choose who we think will be joining us in eternity, as if we were predicting a sports team that hadn't yet been selected, it's to learn to live with everybody *now* and to receive their unexpected gifts with imagination and gratitude in recognition that these are the people with whom we'll be spending eternity, lucky and blessed as we all are to be there, and we'd best use these earthly years as a time for getting in the mood. (Wells, 2019, p. 5 – emphasis added)

This sense of living now, or in what Jean-Pierre de Caussade called the 'sacrament of the present moment', is at the heart of an engaged eschatology and sharing kingdom stories. It is also marked by a keen sense of what might be called 'provisionality'. Warwick Poppies 2018 existed for a relatively short period of time, marking a moment in history. In this book, Chapter 1 began by describing how thrones can be images of power and authority in both popular culture and in hymns. The Iron Throne in the novels and TV series *Game of Thrones* is the seat of dominion and control for the person who rules over the fictitious world of Westeros. It is not much of a spoiler to say that in the final TV episode the throne that many have been seeking to claim throughout the fluctuating storyline is destroyed by a fire-breathing dragon.

And fire is a recurring image for judgement in the Old and New Testaments. In the Gospels it is associated with, among others, John the Baptist's forthright words to the religious authorities (Matthew 3.10–11), with the disciples offering to call down retribution upon a Samaritan village (Luke 9.51–56), and Jesus' words of condemnation on those who cause little ones to stumble (Mark 9.42–48). Fire can often be a biblical metaphor for the arrival of a new age when everything is to be transformed, and this seems to be the way in which it is being used in the conclusion to *Game of Thrones* – a new age will arise from the destruction of the symbol of power. One moment has gone and a new one begins. A story has concluded and another starts.

I have argued in this book that leading ministry requires an engaged eschatology of kingdom stories. By this I mean the storytelling and story-sharing of local churches will weave together narratives from the past and the future but must be fully expressed, lived and told in the present. My contention is that this was how Jesus proclaimed the kingdom of God, and that must be the way for those seeking to follow in his footsteps. In my conclusion I shall present another imagined conversation between Jesus and his disciples before suggesting five ways in which we can identify kingdom stories.

Prayer

God of past, present and future,
in which we live, move and have our being;
we give thanks for our stories
written in the sacrament of the present moment
and told in the eternity of your divine Word;
our praise is offered through the One
who is full of grace and truth. Amen.

On reflection

1 Where do you find kingdom stories within the Church in this 'present moment'?
2 Where do you find kingdom stories outside the Church in this 'present moment'?
3 How does living in the present change your understanding of the past and the future?

Notes

1 Kirstie Smith, 2018, 'Massive community poppy tribute unveiled in Warwick', *The Warwick Courier*, 12 October, www.warwick courier.co.uk/news/massive-community-poppy-tribute-unveiled-in-warwick-1-8666263 (accessed 21.5.19).

2 Kirstie Smith, 2018, 'Here's a selection of photos from the Warwick Poppies community project', *The Warwick Courier*, 15 November, www.warwickcourier.co.uk/news/here-s-a-selection-of-photos-from-the-warwick-poppies-community-project-1-8706633 (accessed 21.5.19).

3 Kirstie Smith, 2019, 'Massive community tribute in Warwick raises thousands of pounds in just nine weeks', *The Warwick Courier*, www.warwickcourier.co.uk/news/massive-community-tribute-in-warwick-raises-thousands-of-pounds-in-just-nine-weeks-1-8819457 (accessed 21.5.19).

4 Kirstie Smith, 2019, 'Warwick Poppies team delighted with first sale days', *The Warwick Courier*, 14 March, www.warwickcourier.co.uk/news/warwick-poppies-team-delighted-with-first-sale-days-1-8848566 (accessed 21.5.19).

5 Kirstie Smith, 2019, 'Accolade for Warwick Poppies project team', *The Warwick Courier*, 22 April, www.warwickcourier.co.uk/news/accolade-for-warwick-poppies-project-team-1-8899579 (accessed 21.5.19).

6 See www.facebook.com/warwickpoppies2018/ and https://twitter.com/WarwickPoppies.

7 For further discussion on how the process of church members, leaders and church communities drawing on their narrative aquifers plays a vital role in how they tell and retell their kingdom stories, see Roberts, 2014.

8 'Life, in fact, is a quality rather than a quantity, and there are certain moments of real life whose value seems so great that to measure them by the clock, and find them to have lasted so many hours or minutes, must appear trivial and meaningless' (quoted in Guiver, 1988, p. 15).

9 Neil Morrissey, Debbie McGee, Ed Byrne, Heather Small, Kate Bottley, Raphael Rowe and JJ Chalmers on 'The Road to Santiago' at www.bbc.co.uk/programmes/b09w7lc8. Les Dennis, Lesley Joseph, Brendan Cole, Stephen K Amos, Katy Brand, Greg Rutherford, Dana and Mehreen Baig 'On the Road to Rome' at www.bbc.co.uk/programmes/m0003wws. Simon Reeve's historical documentaries about pilgrimage can be found on YouTube, for example at www.youtube.com/watch?v=MLkmoHiSIIQ and www.youtube.com/watch?v=Foza JKIVfNU (accessed 30.12.19).

10 The importance of 'counter-stories' is also emphasized by John Swinton (2012, pp. 22–3).

11 The value of transcendence is also made in an article about the challenges faced by secular forms of 'church'. The anthropologist

Richard Sosis notes that while costly sacrifice might not be present in these communities – and they may be suffering for that reason – they have other tools in their toolkit. They already have collective singing and live music, for example, which sets meetings apart from everyday experiences. And he believes they can and will adapt over time, evolving into something closer to conventional religion, even if no deities are involved. Secular congregations can become as meaningful as religious ones, he says, 'but there has to be a sense of transcendence … Transcendence is what gives the community a higher level of meaning than going to Johnny's Little League game.' It might mean developing more rituals, or sharing more stories. It might mean that ideals they already espouse – such as helping others or finding wonder in nature – get elevated to a sacred level. The irony is that to get away from religion, they may need to re-create it. See Faith Hill, 2019, 'They Tried to Start a Church without God', *The Atlantic*, 21 July, www. theatlantic.com/ideas/archive/2019/07/secular-churches-rethink-their-sales-pitch/594109/ (accessed 3.9.19).

12 'Hey Brother' can be found at www.youtube.com/watch?v=6Cp 6mKbRTQY and 'The Nights' can be found at www.youtube.com/ watch?v=UtF6Jej8yb4 (accessed 23.5.19).

13 'Skin' by Rag n Bone Man can be found at www.youtube.com/ watch?v=1Al-nuR1iAU (accessed 23.5.19).

14 Linda Ellis, 'The Dash Poem' © *Inspire Kindness*, 1996, thedash poem.com (accessed 23.5.19).

15 These can be found at www.poemhunter.com/poem/do-not-stand-at-my-grave-and-weep/ and on numerous other sites (accessed 23.5.19).

16 Karen Heller, 2019, 'The funeral as we know it is becoming a relic – just in time for a death boom', *The Washington Post*, 15 April, www.washingtonpost.com/gdpr-consent/?destination=%2flife style%2fstyle%2fthe-funeral-as-we-know-it-is-becoming-a-relic--just-in-time-for-a-death-boom%2f2019%2f04%2f14%2fa49003c4-50c2-11e9-8d28-f5149e5a2fda_story.html%3f&utm_term=.ef3fdafc5f02 (accessed 24.5.19).

17 The final scene has been posted by BBC TV at www.youtube.com/ watch?v=vH3-Gt7mgyM (accessed 24.5.19). On the day I accessed it, this posting had been viewed nearly 3 million times since 2010, which gives an indication of its cultural significance.

18 Sam Wells' lecture for Inclusive Church can be found at www. inclusive-church.org/sites/default/files/files/Sam%20Wells%20IC%20 lecture.pdf (accessed 17.9.19).

Conclusion

Storying the Kingdom

1 A kingdom story

The Introduction to this book started with an imagined conversation between Philip, Bartholomew and Jesus as we began to open up the subject of kingdom stories. As we move towards our conclusion, let me share another story about Jesus talking with his disciples over food and wine.

> Dim lamps flickered as the gentle evening breeze drifted into a room where thirteen people were reclining lazily, having eaten their fill. The wind took liberties – playing with light and shadow on plain, whitewashed walls as the dark and indistinct images of the diners and their dinner. Spectres of people, dishes and goblets – even the bowls for the washing of feet – were thrown on to the white backdrop like a large game of shadow-pictures, seen through a mellow haze of food and drink.
>
> The comfortable silence was broken by one man leaning over to another and saying: 'I really don't understand.'
>
> 'What don't you understand, James?' replied the one being questioned.
>
> James took a while to respond – whether this was because it had been a long and tiring day or because he'd had a little too much wine wasn't clear.
>
> 'Well, Jesus, I don't understand that story you told today about the tenants of the vineyard killing the owner's son and the builders rejecting the keystone.'

Jesus was silent for a while. Then he slowly and deliberately looked at James in the gathering gloom: 'What do *you* think I meant by that?' he asked.

James exploded in exasperation: 'Oh don't start playing those "... and who do you say that I am?" games with us again, Jesus.'

In an effort to ease the growing confrontation, Peter reached for the jug of wine and poured some into James' cup. 'Here you are, James,' he said. 'Stop whining!'

The others groaned loudly. Simon Peter's jokes seemed to get worse as time went by.

'No, I want to know,' continued James pushing the goblet away. 'Did you mean that God's going to reject our temple and reject all the sacrifices that we've been making there?'

Jesus filled his own cup and took a sip. 'There's nothing wrong in not understanding something,' he said. 'If we want to know what our temple and sacrifices are truly about, then we've to go back to Abraham and Isaac, haven't we? You know, when Abraham was called by God to go and sacrifice his only son, I'm sure that Abraham didn't understand then – didn't have the first clue, I should think. But then life, faith, God are like that sometimes – sometimes they don't seem to make sense at all. And, sometimes, we are all called to give up something that's very precious to us; something we love dearly, beyond anything else, and I suppose that, in the end, we have to remember that we don't have anything, anything, not even a child or a relationship, that wasn't given to us by God in the first place.'

The darkness seemed to gather and thicken at this point, as they sat in a moment of silence. James shuffled uncomfortably. 'Yes, but does it matter about the temple and our sacrifices any more?'

Jesus didn't reply but looked at the discarded plates and cups left from their meal. Again Peter tried to ease his own sense of discomfort. He picked up a shallow dish with a bit of meat left on it and offered it to James. 'Trouble with you,

James, is that you want everything given you on a plate.' But no one even groaned this time.

Eventually Jesus stirred. 'Yes, the temple and our sacrifices do matter,' he said quietly. 'The sacrifices of our hearts in the temples of our bodies – that's why we've been baptized. Our bodies are the buildings that need to be dedicated to God, and our hearts and our actions are the sacrifices that we make there.'

He paused. 'But it's just the same as with Abraham and Isaac really. Our hearts and our actions shrink to nothing when put alongside all that God has done for us and the great love that God has for each of us individually. God cares for the whole of creation – the tiniest sparrow, each hair on our head – right the way up to the big things in life. So big that sometimes they're beyond our understanding. That's one of the things that being baptized is all about – a sign of God's love poured out on the world in all its enormous complexity and a sign of God's love poured out for each one of us however small we may feel.'

The thirteen diners sat silently thinking about the time they'd been baptized, until James hesitantly but persistently said: 'So ... what about the Temple in Jerusalem?'

Slowly Jesus lifted his head and looked round the table at each one of them in turn, as if assessing them individually. Eventually he responded: 'Well ... it's still standing. But maybe we'd better go there sometime, and overturn a few of the ideas that people have about that place.'

And with those words the remaining twelve had that familiar churning feeling in their stomachs and a familiar phrase sprang into each of their minds: 'Now, what exactly did he *mean* by that?'

I write stories such as these for liturgical purposes, to illuminate the world in which Jesus lived and to encourage listeners to reflect anew on the Gospel accounts. I also enjoy reading and evaluating those written about Jesus by others. In my view, a good example is Gerd Theissen's *The Shadow of the Galilean*

(1987), whereas Philip Pullman's *The Good Man Jesus and the Scoundrel Christ* (2010) did not – for me, at least – succeed in opening up a credible imaginative world that shed new light on Jesus' story. As we noted at the outset, many storytellers have tried their hand at reworking the story of Jesus, and they are one form of what I am calling a kingdom story.

In this instance, the imagined conversation between Jesus, James and Peter is designed to bring to mind some of the discussions about kingdom stories from the first two chapters in this book, as well as pointing towards the inherent connections between kingdom stories and quests for meaning examined in Chapters 3 and 4.

However, the notion of an engaged eschatology explored throughout this study suggests that kingdom stories can take many different forms, so I want to conclude by offering five ways in which such stories can be identified.

2 How do we identify kingdom stories?

(i) Kingdom stories embody God's action in our world

We considered this in Chapter 1, before outlining four of the most significant approaches to Jesus' eschatology when we noted Gustaf Dalman's understanding that Jesus spoke about God's kingdom as a way of highlighting God's action in the world. I argued that the three artistic illustrations discussed at that point – Alfie Bradley's sculpted *Knife Angel*, Francis Thompson's poetic 'The Kingdom of God' and Greta Gerwig's cinematic *Lady Bird* – all provide a sense of God's action in our world in the present moment. Chapter 4 provided a detailed study of an example from the practical ministry of one local church. Warwick Poppies 2018 illustrates different forms of improvised story (Roberts and Sims, 2017, ch. 8) and how they can manifest themselves in a specific project.

Alongside this lived experience of one kingdom story we have also drawn on how similar ideas are being explored by other theologians and clergy. For instance, through a series of books, Sam Wells has challenged the Church to take seriously the idea of being 'with' (Wells, 2015, 2017, 2018), which is also a significant element in John Swinton's conclusion to his book about dementia (Swinton, 2012), where he stresses the importance of 'visitation' and being with those who are sick. Commenting on the Lord's Prayer, he writes: 'When God's will is done, heaven is revealed' (p. 286). I agree with this statement and would add that by undertaking 'visitation' and being 'with', we are modelling the way of the incarnation and the divine nature of our Creator, which is to be with us in the experiences discussion – facing up to knife crime, walking by the River Thames, reflecting on broken relationships and how they can be mended, and all of life's events and encounters.

A second way to enter into kingdom stories and to recognize them is through the pattern of the incarnate Christ himself and all that he shared through his life, death and resurrection, which we considered in Chapters 1 and 2.

(ii) They can relate directly to Jesus' parables, teaching and lived example

Chapter 2 explored a number of Jesus' parables (the farmer and the seed, the cost of building a tower and going to war, the talents), his actions (temptations in the wilderness, calling the disciples, washing the disciples' feet) and his teaching (about himself and his calling, and wisdom, meaning and discernment). I linked those Gospel accounts to our contemporary world through a series of terms that are part of present-day organizational and church culture: typologies, purpose, discipleship for the parables; risk, followership, trust for actions; and purpose and discipleship for teaching.

When people make connections with the stories of Jesus' life in all their rich diversity, they are engaging with kingdom stories. This may come through listening to a 'Thought for the Day' on the radio or hearing a sermon on Remembrance Sunday, through meeting someone who is living their vocation or reading an article or book, through hearing a moving piece of music or attending a Bible study. In and through such direct encounters with Jesus' continuing presence, we too enter into kingdom stories.

In *So What's the Story …?*, Clive Marsh puts it this way:

> When we tell the story of Jesus we are linking back to the historical figure of Jesus. But we are also saying something about God. The claim that God was in, and with, Jesus in a unique way affects how the story is told. We are saying something about ourselves too: wanting to tell Jesus-stories we are suggesting how and why he has an impact upon us, folding into our tale implicitly or explicitly aspects of the kind of faith we hold. (Glasson and Marsh, 2019, p. 76)

We can perceive kingdom stories through immediate encounters with the traditions about Jesus but there are also more unforeseen, even accidental, encounters. These may be deeply embedded narratives that become part of our vocational story about risk and discipleship or they may be flashes of insight such as Ann Lewin's poem about the kingfisher. Nevertheless, there are ways in which the kingdom stories about Jesus connect directly with our lives and bring moments of engaged eschatology into our world. The process of leading in this context requires us to remain open at all times to the in-breaking of these stories.

(iii) They can relate indirectly to Jesus' parables, teaching and lived example

One of the things that has emerged clearly from these discussions is that the Gospel accounts about Jesus and kingdom stories themselves are not fixed in aspic. They have a life of their own that requires, as I have just said, engagement and interpretation. Clive Marsh identifies one of the dangers in this respect when people believe that the Christian story provides a script, which in turn can give the impression that:

> All we need to do, then, is learn the script ('do this, do that') and all manner of things will be well. Certain words and convictions, particular actions, specific beliefs can all be adopted and practiced and then the task of 'living the Gospel' can be achieved by 'inhabiting the script'. As Christians, we are, it may be assumed, actors who live according to God's script. Our job is to slot into what God has laid out, learn the lines and perform the play. (Glasson and Marsh, 2019, p. 131)

By contrast, he contends that we participate in God's story and our performance requires improvisation. At this point he moves away from the metaphor of script and introduces the image of jazz, seeing our narrative involvement as musical improvisation. Although I can see what he is trying to get at, I would prefer to stay with the idea of story and script. One person who has done a great deal of work on how scripts work in communal settings is Iain L. Mangham. He argues that in organizations:

> The acquisition of the script itself is to be seen as a creative process in the sense that interpretations of events, relations, and situations are not predetermined in a fixed way for all time by any particular culture, although such interpretations may *appear* to be limited by conventional usage. (Mangham, 1978, p. 25 – emphasis original)

In their book *Organizations as Theatre* (1987), Iain Mangham and Michael Overington develop the notion of how scripts, drama and performance can be developed creatively in different social settings. Simon Walker has applied this metaphor to leadership, saying that a leader is similar to a theatre director: 'She needs to be the one who draws the "story arc" of the whole community. She may leave it to her cast to develop the script themselves, but she takes responsibility for the trajectory of the story' (Walker, 2011, p. 318). In other words, improvisation is as important in scripts as in, say, jazz.[1]

The key point here is that scripts and stories are inherently more flexible than Marsh suggests and can take on a life of their own. Thus, themes from kingdom stories and kingdom stories themselves can be found beyond the bounds of the Church, embedded in local communities and wider artistic and popular culture. The role of churches is not to 'claim' or 'own' such narratives but to recognize where they are being told and to encourage and enhance the storytelling. My contention is that the Warwick Poppies provides a good example of finding kingdom stories in the world and drawing them into an open and healthy relationship with the Church. The script for Warwick Poppies was improvised around kingdom themes in order to create a kingdom story.

(iv) They can often be about sense-making and seeking meaning

At the time of writing, a delightful news story emerged about a tourist who went missing on a sightseeing trip in Iceland, only to be found as one of the members of the search party. She was part of a group travelling by coach that stopped to look at a volcanic canyon. Soon there was word of a missing passenger, and the woman, who for some reason had changed her clothes, didn't recognize the description being given out and joined in the search. It was eventually called off at three in the morning when it became clear that the missing passenger was accounted for and had been searching for herself! One of the reasons why that story appealed to me is that it seems to encapsulate something of the surprise that sense-making can involve, and there are echoes here of the folk tale in Chapter 2.2 about the traveller searching for the heavenly city. Quite often the best place to find a sense of meaning is where we are in the present.

Indeed, the human drive to make sense of our experiences and find meaning in our lives has been a recurring theme in this book. It is referenced in my concluding short story but we explored this idea in Chapter 2 (particularly 2.7, 'Kingdom stories, wisdom and meaning'. Chapter 3 looked at processes of sense-making in different forms of art (the frescoes of Signorelli, the sermon/poetry of Henry Scott Holland and the films *The Shape of Water* and *Coco*. And, in Chapter 4, I have argued that a knitted poppies project and twenty-first-century acts of remembrance also illustrate this fundamental characteristic of kingdom stories.

David Sims and I discuss meaning and stories in *Leading by Story*, and at one point David observes: 'Stories are what gives meaning to events' (Roberts and Sims, 2017, p. 77). Engaged eschatology will always be seeking meaning and the purposes of God in the narratives that we share. A crucial element in leading a local church will be providing resources and opportunities for people to seek and find meaning in their personal and communal storytelling.

(v) They can often challenge individuals and communities

Chapter 2 discussed how Jesus' kingdom stories could be challenging, especially (but not only) those about risk, trust, discipleship and authenticity. At the start of his ministry, Jesus makes it clear that the prophet Isaiah is a vital part of his story:

> The scroll of the prophet Isaiah was given to him. He unrolled the scroll and found the place where it was written:
>
> > The Spirit of the Lord is upon me,
> > because he has anointed me to bring good news to
> > the poor.
> > He has sent me to proclaim release to the captives
> > and recovery of sight to the blind,
> > to let the oppressed go free,
> > to proclaim the year of the Lord's favour.'
>
> And he rolled up the scroll, gave it back to the attendant, and sat down. The eyes of all in the synagogue were fixed on him. Then he began to say to them, 'Today this scripture has been fulfilled in your hearing.' (Luke 4.17–21)

At the conclusion to his discussion about the growth of what is now Isaiah's prophecy and in his summary of prophecy as a whole within the Old Testament, John Barton argues:

> The prophetic books, like the pieces of which they are composed, are for the most part subversive entities, undercutting the foundations of established religion, especially the state religious cults of the Hebrew kingdoms in pre-exilic times, and the political machinations of the times just before the exile. (Barton, 2019, p. 111)

He goes on to say that the prophetic message was domesticated by later Judaism, and although Christianity heard their critical messages, it mainly saw them as proclaiming a coming new age of hope.

Barton is right to warn against the taming of prophetic challenge that can exist in Judaism, Christianity and other walks of life, faith and culture. I would argue that Jesus takes up the challenge of Isaiah and other prophets in seeking and proclaiming signs of God's kingdom. The most profound revelation of that search is in Jesus' kingdom story of cross and empty tomb. Sam Wells relates that to life of the ongoing Body of Christ when he states that whenever a community acts in such a way

> that their gestures point back to the transforming events of death and resurrection and point forward to the eschatological fulfilment of God's promises, their actions may be described as prophetic. The point of a prophetic action is not to change the world but to display the manner in which the world is changed by God. (Wells, 2006, p. 203)

I agree that the engaged eschatology we see revealed in Jesus' sacrifice and vindication offers promise and hope, as Wells suggests, but I believe it is also a call to seek change in our world as well. That change can include ourselves, our immediate circumstances, our local community, our nation and further afield. Stories of change are kingdom stories.

Note

1 For more on improvisation and interpretation in organizations, see Weick, 2001, chapter 3, and for more on poetics and meaning in theology, see Dyrness, 2011, chapter 1.

3 Kingdom stories: telling, leading, discerning

Jesus urged his first hearers to listen and look for signs of God's kingdom as he declared that those signs were all around for those who could discern God's action in the world. In this book I have argued that such a gospel insight remains as true now as it did in the first century. It is the process of finding the presence of God in the multitude and complexity of our stories that I am calling engaged eschatology. This engagement with kingdom stories can happen inside and outside church ministry and the various forms in which local ministry is apparent.

In the conclusion to *Leading by Story*, David Sims and I observed that 'leading needs to involve enabling people to tell their stories, hearing the stories that are being told, and enabling others to hear the stories too' (Roberts and Sims, 2017, p. 199). The action of leading in terms of kingdom stories involves the process of encouraging others to tell their kingdom stories as well as recounting our own. As we recognize (discern) stories of God at work, Christian communities and individuals are called to be at the heart (leading) of sharing those stories (telling) as signs of good news for testing and demanding times.

Afterword

by the Rt Revd Professor Christopher Herbert

On Christmas Eve 2015, the BBC, following an initiative taken by Norwegian TV a few years earlier, decided to broadcast a two-hour-long television programme. It followed two young Sami women trekking through the snow-covered landscape of northern Norway. There was no voice-over, no gimmicks, no background music, just two people crunching through snow with a reindeer-pulled sledge. It was beautiful and vividly memorable.

The concept of slowness has been, forgive the phrase, slowly developing. In 1999, in Italy, the concept of Slow Towns was developed at Greve in Chianti, Tuscany. Since then, Slow Towns have sprung up across the world. In the UK, Aylsham in Norfolk is one such, as is also Ludlow in Shropshire. The idea behind the movement is that life has become for many people so frantic that what makes life worth living is squeezed to the margins. The Slow Town movement seeks to restore humane and precious values to our streets.

I have a sneaking suspicion that this book falls into a similar category. It is profound, full of insights discovered in contemporary film and novels, and, perhaps more unexpectedly, in theories of organizational change and in theology. By weaving these normally separate categories deftly together with biblical material, Vaughan Roberts has produced a work that is wise and wonderfully enriching. But ... it needs to be savoured, to be taken slowly, so that its underlying messages can be quietly pondered and its implications inhabited.

Any church leader, bombarded with the slogans that seem to emanate so frantically from the central parts of ecclesiastical life, should simply ignore them and instead read this book, preferably in the company of parishioners; for I am sure that such an activity would be transformative and life-giving.

By concentrating on the centrality of the kingdom in Jesus' life and teaching, and by exploring the challenging, radical and vivacious change of mind that such stories engender, Vaughan Roberts has drawn on his huge pastoral experience to bring out some of the implications for contemporary society. His love of stories shines through – and we should not forget that stories cannot be rushed. They are to be enjoyed and internalized so that our perceptions of the world and of God are changed and refreshed.

If, in the future, a movement begins calling itself 'Slow Theology', its proponents might look back on this book as one of its major starting points.

It deserves to be widely read, partly because it is a joy in itself, but also because its central theme really does have the potential to change the direction of travel of those individuals and groups who read it.

You might have guessed that I loved it and count it a privilege to be able to commend it.

The Rt Revd Professor Christopher Herbert
Visiting Professor of Christian Ethics, University of Surrey and formerly Bishop of St Albans

Bibliography and Further Reading

Alvesson, M. and A. Spicer, 2011, *Metaphors We Lead By: Understanding Leadership in the Real World*, London and New York: Routledge.

Barbour, R. S., 2000, 'Kingdom of God', in Adrian Hastings, Alistair Mason and Hugh Pyper (eds), *The Oxford Companion to Christian Thought: Intellectual, Spiritual, and Moral Horizons of Christianity*, Oxford and New York: Oxford University Press, pp. 370–1.

Barton, John, 2019, *A History of the Bible: The Book and its Faiths*, London: Allen Lane.

Bassett, Debra J., 2015, 'Who Wants to Live Forever? Living, Dying and Grieving in Our Digital Society', *Social Sciences* 4, pp. 1127–39, and available online at https://warwick.academia.edu/DebbieBassett (accessed 21.5.19).

Bassett, Debra J., 2018a, 'Ctrl+Alt+Delete: The Changing Landscape of the Uncanny Valley and the Fear of Second Loss', in *Current Psychology* (September 2018) and available online at https://warwick.academia.edu/DebbieBassett (accessed 21.5.19).

Bassett, Debra J., 2018b, 'Digital Afterlives: From Social Media Platforms to Thanabots and Beyond', in Charles Tandy (ed.), *Death and Anti-Death, Vol. 16: Two Hundred Years after Frankenstein*, Ann Arbor, MI: Ria University Press, and available online at https://warwick.academia.edu/DebbieBassett (accessed 21.5.19).

Bauckham, Richard, 2000, 'Eschatology', in Adrian Hastings, Alistair Mason and Hugh Pyper (eds), *The Oxford Companion to Christian Thought: Intellectual, Spiritual, and Moral Horizons of Christianity*, Oxford and New York: Oxford University Press, pp. 206–9.

Brindley, David, 2001, *Richard Beauchamp: Medieval England's Greatest Knight*, Stroud and Charleston, SC: Tempus Publishing.

Brown, David, 2000, *Discipleship and Imagination: Christian Tradition and Truth*, Oxford: Oxford University Press.

Burridge, Richard A., 2004, *What are the Gospels? A Comparison with Graeco-Roman Biography*, 2nd edn, Grand Rapids, MI: Eerdmans.

Cable, Daniel M., 2018, *Alive at Work: The Neuroscience of Helping Your People Love What They Do*, Boston, MA: Harvard Business Review Press.

Carroll, Jackson W., 2011, *As One with Authority: Reflective Leadership in Ministry*, 2nd edn, Eugene, OR: Cascade Books.

Chartered Institute of Personnel and Development (CIPD) and University of Bath, 2014a, *Cultivating Trustworthy Leaders*, London: CIPD.

Chartered Institute of Personnel and Development (CIPD) and University of Bath, 2014b, *Experiencing Trustworthy Leadership*, London: CIPD.

Countryman, L. William, 1999, *Living on the Border of the Holy: Renewing the Priesthood of All*, Harrisburg, PA: Morehouse Publishing.

Craddock, Fred, 2001, *Craddock Stories*, ed. Mike Graves and Richard F. Wards, St Louis, MO: Chalice Press.

Cullmann, Oscar, 1963, *The Christology of the New Testament*, 2nd edn, London: SCM Press.

de Mello SJ, Anthony, 1989, *The Prayer of the Frog*, vol. 2, Anand, India: Gujarat Sahitya Prakash.

Denning, Steve, 2011, *The Leader's Guide to Storytelling: Mastering the Art and Discipline of Business Narrative*, San Francisco, CA: Jossey-Bass.

Dennis, Trevor, 2003, *The Book of Books: The Bible Retold*, Oxford: Lion Books.

Dietz, Graham and Deanne N. Den Hartog, 2006, 'Measuring Trust Inside Organizations', *Personnel Review* 35:5, pp. 557–88.

Dodd, C. H., 1961, *The Parables of the Kingdom*, rev. edn, Glasgow: Collins.

Dodd, C. H., 1968, *The Interpretation of the Fourth Gospel*, Cambridge: Cambridge University Press.

Dodd, C. H., 1976, *Historical Tradition in the Fourth Gospel*, Cambridge: Cambridge University Press.

Dulles, Avery, 1978, *Models of the Church*, New York: Doubleday Image Books.

Dunn, James D. G., 1980, *Christology in the Making: A New Testament Inquiry into the Doctrine of the Incarnation*, Philadelphia, PA: Westminster Press.

Dyrness, William A., 2011, *Poetic Theology: God and the Poetics of Everyday Life*, Grand Rapids, MI: Eerdmans Publishing.

Etchells, Ruth, 1998, *A Reading of the Parables of Jesus*, London: Darton, Longman and Todd.

Fineman, Stephen, David Sims and Yiannis Gabriel, 2005, *Organizing and Organizations*, 3rd edn, London: Sage.

Fitzmaurice, John, 2016, *Virtue Ecclesiology: An Exploration in the Good Church*, Farnham and Burlington, VT: Ashgate Publishing.

Franklin, Eric, 2001, 'Luke', in *The Oxford Bible Commentary*, ed. John Barton and John Muddiman, Oxford: Oxford University Press, pp. 922–59.

Gabriel, Yiannis, 1993, 'On Organizational Nostalgia – Reflections on "The Golden Age"', originally published in S. Fineman (ed.), *Emotion in Organizations*, London: Sage, pp. 118–41, and available online at www.yiannisgabriel.com/2014/01/on-organizational-nostalgia-reflections.html (accessed 21.5.19).

Gabriel, Yiannis, 2000, *Organizational Storytelling: Facts, Fictions, Fantasies*, Oxford: Oxford University Press.

Gabriel, Yiannis, 2016, 'Narrative Ecologies and the Role of Counter-Narratives: The Case of Nostalgic Stories and Conspiracy Theories', in Sanne Frandsen, Timothy Kuhn and Marianne Wolff Lundholt (eds), *Counter-narratives and Organization*, London: Routledge, pp. 208–26.

Galford, Robert and Anne Seibold Drapeau, 2002, *The Trusted Leader: Bringing Out the Best in Your People and Your Company*, New York: The Free Press.

Gawande, Atul, 2014, *Being Mortal: Illness, Medicine and What Matters in the End*, London: Profile Books.

Glasson, Barbara and Clive Marsh, 2019, *So What's the Story …? A Resource Book for Christian Reflection and Practice*, London: Darton, Longman and Todd.

Goffee, Rob and Gareth Jones, 2006, *Why Should Anyone be Led by You? What it Takes to be an Authentic Leader*, Boston, MA: Harvard Business School Press.

Gooder, Paula, 2018, *Phoebe: A Story (with Notes) – Pauline Christianity in Narrative Form*, London: Hodder and Stoughton.

Gore, Charles, 1890, *Lux Mundi: A Series of Studies in the Religion of the Incarnation*, 10th edn, London: John Murray.

Guiver, George, 1988, *Company of Voices: Daily Prayer and the People of God*, London: SPCK.

Hengel, Martin, 2004, *Studies in Early Christology*, London and New York: T & T Clark.

Hurst, David K., 2012, *The New Ecology of Leadership: Business Mastery in a Chaotic World*, New York and Chichester: Columbia Business School.

Hybels, Bill, 2002, *Courageous Leadership*, Grand Rapids, MI: Zondervan.

James, Sara Nair, 2003, *Signorelli and Fra Angelico at Orvieto: Liturgy, Poetry and a Vision of the End-Time*, Aldershot and Burlington, VT: Ashgate Publishing.

Katz, Daniel and Robert L. Kahn, 1978, *The Social Psychology of Organizations*, 2nd edn, New York and Chichester: John Wiley & Sons.

Kellerman, Barbara, 2008, *Followership: How Followers are Creating Change and Changing Leaders*, Boston, MA: Harvard Business Review Press.

Kostera, Monika, 2012, *Organizations and Archetypes*, Cheltenham and Northampton, MA: Edward Elgar.

Lamdin, Keith, 2012, *Finding Your Leadership Style: A Guide for Ministers*, London: SPCK.

Lewin, Ann, 1990, *By the Way*, Southampton: Ann Lewin.

MacCulloch, Diarmaid, 2018, *Thomas Cromwell: A Life*, London: Allen Lane.

McLellan, Dugald, 1998, *Signorelli's Orvieto Frescoes: A Guide to the Cappella Nuova of Orvieto Cathedral*, Ponte San Giovanni, Perugia: Quattroemme Srl.

MacMillan, Margaret, 2001, *Peacemakers: The Paris Conference of 1919 and its Attempt to End War*, London: John Murray.

Mangham, Iain L., 1978, *Interactions and Interventions in Organizations*, Chichester and New York: John Wiley & Sons.

Mangham, Iain L. and Michael A. Overington, 1987, *Organizations as Theatre: A Social Psychology of Dramatic Appearances*, Chichester and New York: John Wiley & Sons.

Mannix, Kathryn, 2017, *With the End in Mind: Dying, Death and Wisdom in an Age of Denial*, London: William Collins.

Manson, T. W., 1949, *The Sayings of Jesus*, London: SCM Press.

Marsh, Clive and Steve Moyise, 2015, *Jesus and the Gospels: An Introduction*, 3rd edn, London: Bloomsbury.

Marsh, Clive and Vaughan S. Roberts, 2015, 'Listening as Religious Practice (Part Two) – Exploring Qualitative Data from an Empirical Study of Music Fans', *Journal of Contemporary Religion* 30:2, pp. 291–306.

Marsh, Clive, 2018, *A Cultural Theology of Salvation*, Oxford: Oxford University Press.

Mayer, Roger C., James H. Davis and F. David Schoorman, 1995, 'An Integrative Model of Organizational Trust', *Academy of Management Review* 20:3, pp. 709–34.

Mead, Geoff, 2014, *Telling the Story: The Heart and Soul of Successful Leadership*, San Francisco, CA and Chichester: Jossey-Bass.

Mintzberg, Henry, Bruce Ahlstrand and Joseph Lampel, 1998, *Strategy Safari: The Complete Guide through the Wilds of Strategic Management*, London and New York: Financial Times/Prentice Hall.

Moreau, A. Scott, 2018, *Contextualizing the Faith: A Holistic Approach*, Grand Rapids, MI: Baker Academic.

Morgan, Gareth, 1997, *Images of Organization*, 2nd edn, Thousand Oaks, CA and London: Sage.

Morisy, Ann, 2004, *Journeying Out: A New Approach to Christian Mission*, London and New York: Continuum.

Nicholls, David, 1989, *Deity and Domination: Images of God and the State in the Nineteenth and Twentieth Centuries*, London and New York: Routledge.

Niebuhr, H. Richard, 1951, *Christ and Culture*, New York: Harper & Row.

Perrin, Nicholas, 2018, *Jesus the Priest*, Grand Rapids, MI: Baker Academic.

Preston, Ronald H., 1983, *Church and Society in the Late Twentieth Century: The Economic and Political Task*, London: SCM Press.

Pritchard, John, 2001, *Living the Gospel Stories Today*, London: SPCK.

Pullman, Philip, 2010, *The Good Man Jesus and the Scoundrel Christ*, Edinburgh: Canongate Books.

Roberts, Vaughan S., 2000, 'A Body of Consensus? The Church as Embodied Organization', in G. R. Evans and Martyn Percy (eds), *Managing the Church: Order and Organization in a Secular Age*, Sheffield: Sheffield Academic Press, pp. 153–73.

Roberts, Vaughan S., 2008, 'Learning What Kind of Leader You Are', in John Nelson (ed.), *How to Become a Creative Church Leader*, Norwich: Canterbury Press, pp. 15–25.

Roberts, Vaughan S., 2014, 'Aquifer Analysis: Told and Untold Stories in Warwick Churches', in Michael Izak, Linda Hitchin and David Anderson (eds), *Untold Stories in Organizations*, New York and London: Routledge, pp. 169–89.

Roberts, Vaughan S., 2017a, 'Folk Music', in Christopher Partridge and Marcus Moberg (eds), *The Bloomsbury Handbook of Religion and Popular Music*, London and New York: Bloomsbury, pp. 260–8.

Roberts, Vaughan S., 2017b, *The Power of Story to Change a Church*, Cambridge: Grove Books.

Roberts, Vaughan S. and David Sims, 2017, *Leading by Story: Rethinking Church Leadership*, London: SCM Press.

Rohr, Richard, 1997, *Yes and … Daily Meditations*, Cincinnati, OH: Franciscan Media.

Rowell, Geoffrey, 2015, 'Henry Scott Holland (1847–1918): Life and Context', *International Journal for the Study of the Christian Church* 15:1, pp. 1–6.

Royce, Josiah, 1908, *The Philosophy of Loyalty*, New York: Macmillan.

Rutter, Esther, 2019, *This Golden Fleece: A Journey through Britain's Knitted History*, London: Granta.

Sachs, William L., 1993, *The Transformation of Anglicanism: From State Church to Global Communion*, Cambridge and New York: Cambridge University Press.

Sadgrove, Michael, 2008, *Wisdom and Ministry: The Call to Leadership*, London: SPCK.

Sanders, E. P., 1985, *Jesus and Judaism*, London: SCM Press.

Schwarz, Hans, 2000, *Eschatology*, Grand Rapids, MI and Cambridge: Eerdmans.

Schweitzer, Albert, 1954, *The Quest of the Historical Jesus: A Critical*

Study of its Progress from Reimarus to Wrede, 3rd edn, London: SCM Press.

Smith, James K. A., 2013, *Imagining the Kingdom: How Worship Works*, Grand Rapids, MI: Baker Academic.

Spoelstra, Sverre, 2018, *Leadership and Organization: A Philosophical Introduction*, Abingdon and New York: Routledge.

Swinton, John, 2012, *Dementia: Living in the Memories of God*, London: SCM Press.

Theissen, Gerd, 1987, *The Shadow of the Galilean: The Quest of the Historical Jesus in Narrative Form*, London: SCM Press.

Theissen, Gerd, 1992, *The Gospels in Context: Social and Political History in the Synoptic Tradition*, Edinburgh: T & T Clark.

Thompson, Jim, 1991, *Stepney Calling: Thoughts for Our Day*, ed. Paul Handley, London: Mowbray.

Underhill, Evelyn, 1940, *Abba: Meditations on the Lord's Prayer*, London: Longmans, Green & Co.

Walker, Simon P., 2011, *The Undefended Leader Trilogy: An Odyssey across the Frontiers of Leadership*, Human Ecology Partners.

Warner, Martin, 2009, *Between Heaven and Charing Cross: Finding a Way to Faith*, London: Mowbray.

Watson, J. R. (ed.), 2002, *An Annotated Anthology of Hymns*, Oxford and New York: Oxford University Press.

Weick, Karl E., 2001, *Making Sense of the Organization*, Oxford and Malden, MA: Blackwell Publishers.

Wells, Samuel, 2006 *God's Companions: Reimagining Christian Ethics*, Oxford: Blackwell Publishing.

Wells, Samuel, 2015, *A Nazareth Manifesto: Being with God*, Chichester and Malden, MA: John Wiley & Sons.

Wells, Samuel, 2017, *Incarnational Ministry: Being with the Church*, London: Canterbury Press.

Wells, Samuel, 2018, *Incarnational Mission: Being with the World*, London: Canterbury Press.

Wells, Samuel, 2019, 'Citizens of Heaven: Identity, Inclusion and the Church', Inclusive Church Annual Lecture, Southwark Cathedral, 9 July 2019, www.inclusive-church.org/sites/default/files/files/Sam%20 Wells%20IC%20lecture.pdf.

White, William R., 1986, *Stories for Telling: A Treasury for Christian Storytellers*, Minneapolis, MN: Augsburg.

Witherington III, Ben, 1995, *The Jesus Quest: The Third Search for the Jew of Nazareth*, Carlisle: Paternoster Press.

Witherington III, Ben and Christopher Mead Armitage, 2002, *The Poetry of Piety: An Annotated Anthology of Christian Poetry*, Grand Rapids, MI: Baker Academic.

Wright, N. T., 1996, *Jesus and the Victory of God*, London: SPCK.

Index of Biblical References

Genesis
32.22–32   50

Exodus
3.11   25
34.28   24

Numbers
14.33–34   28

Judges
7.2–23   53

1 Kings
19.8   25
19.10, 14   25

Ecclesiastes
3.1–8   121

Isaiah
26.19   59
29.18   59
35.5–6   59
42.7, 18   59
61.1   59

Matthew
2.13–23   28
3.10–11   128
4.1–11   21, 23–29

11.2–19   21, 58–64
17.1–8   25, 34
18.3   27
20.20–28   34
22.1–14   75
25.14–30   21, 65–71
25.31–46   68
27.27–28   35
27.29   25
28.20

Mark
1.16–20   21, 30–38
3.13–14   34
5.18–19   35
8.27–38   21, 46–51, 76
9.2–8   25, 34
9.42–48   128
10.21   34
13.5–6   87
14.3–3   75
15.36   25

Luke
1.26–38   28
2.1–7   28
4.15–26   25, 141
5.27–32   74
7.31–35   62
8.4–15   21, 39–45

8.38–39   35
9.28–36   25, 34
9.51–56   128
10.1–2   34
12.1   53
14.25–33   21, 52–57
15.11–32   75
19.1–10   34, 75
20.9–18   53
22.26–27   73

John
2.1–11   77
8.1–11   35
13.3–16   21, 72–79
17.12   87

Acts 2   70

2 Thessalonians
2.3–4   86–87

1 John
2.18, 22   86
4.3   86

2 John
7   86

Revelation
11.3   88

Index of Names and Subjects

Acoustic axes 84
Aesop's fables 63, 78–79
Ahlstrand, Bruce 42
*All hail the power of Jesus'
    name* 2
Alvesson, Mats 42
Alzheimer's Awareness Day 113
Andersen, Hans Christian 63
Angel voices ever singing 1
Antichrist 86–92, 97–100
April Fool's Day 113
Aquifer, storytelling metaphor 3,
    56, 130
Armistice Day 107, 118, 126
Armitage, Christopher Mead 13
Aston Villa F.C. 119
Atlantic, The 131
Avicii (Tim Bergling) 119, 131

Barbour, R. S. 5
Barton, John 80, 121–122, 141
Bassett, Debra 108–109, 113
Bauckham, Richard 9
Biblical stories, retelling xiii–xvi,
    132–135
Blackadder Goes Forth 123–124
Blood Swept Lands and Seas, The
    107
Boden, Richard 123
Bonhoeffer, Dietrich 84, 91–92,
    98–100, 112, 124
Boyle, Danny 89
Bosley, Scott 'Boz' 119–120, 123
Bradley, Alfie 10–11, 20, 136

Brindley, David 104
Brown, David 68
Burridge, Richard 80
Buy Your Priest A Beer
    Day 113–114

Cain and Abel 88
Carroll, Jackson W. 18
Chartered Institute of Personnel
    and Development 75–77
Clifton, Don 42
Cable, Daniel 53–56
Cocksworth, Christopher ix,
    xi–xii, 10–11
Coventry Cathedral 10–11, 20
Chaucer, Geoffrey 104
Coco xviii, 83, 94–95, 140
Countryman, L. William 35
Craddock, Fred 69–70
Cranmer, Thomas 45
Cullmann, Oscar 7
Cummins, Paul 107
Cunningham, Amy 120

Dalman, Gustaf 5
Dash, the 119, 131
Davies, J. H. 79
Death is nothing at all xviii
Da Vinci, Leonardo 85
de Caussade, Jean-Pierre 128
della Francesca, Piero 85
del Toro, Guillermo 94
de Mello, Anthony 78
Denning, Stephen 17, 66, 70

Dennis, Trevor xvi
Denver, Colorado 7
Dickens, Charles xvi
Dietz, Graham 79
Divine Comedy, The 87
Dodd, C. H. 6, 73–74
Do not stand at my grave and
    weep 119, 131
Drapeau, Anne Seibold 27
Dulles, Avery 41, 43
Dunn, James D. G. 62
Dyrness, William A. 142

Edward VII, King 94
Economist, The 111
Elijah, Prophet 25–26, 63, 90, 99
Ellis, Linda 119
Enoch, Prophet 90, 99
Eschatology xvii–xviii, 9
    engaged xviii, 3–4, 9, 12–14,
    37, 80–81, 88–101, 103, 110,
    127–130, 137–142
    imminent or apocalyptic 5–6,
    101, 104
    inaugurated 7
    realized 6–7, 104
    restoration 7–8, 65
Etchells, Ruth 2–3, 52–53, 63

FA Cup 114
Fitzmaurice, John 16, 43
Fra Angelico 85–88
Fry, Mary Elizabeth 119

Gabriel, Yiannis 21, 40, 110–112
Galford, Robert 27
Game of Thrones 1, 10, 128–129
Gawande, Atul 115–118
Gerwig, Greta 14, 136
Glasson, Barbara 102–103,
    137–138
Goffee, Rob 47–50
Golden Legend, The 87
Gooder, Paula xvi
Gore, Charles 93

Graham, Billy 30
Guiver, George 113–114

Hartog, Deanne Den 79
Haüerwas, Stanley 125
Hengel, Martin 63, 91
Herbert, Christopher ix,
    144–145
Holland, Henry Scott xviii, 83,
    93–96, 98, 140
Hurst, David 60–62
Hybels, Bill 42, 45

Ibarra, Herminia 47–50
Isaiah, Prophet 59, 63, 141

James, Sara Nair 86, 90
Jazz 138
Jerusalem Temple, The xvii, 27,
    55, 58, 69–70, 76, 90, 99–100,
    103, 138–139
Jones, Gareth 47–50

Kahn, Robert L. 40, 44
Katz, Daniel 40, 44
Kellerman, Barbara 32–35, 42
Kerouac, Jack 7
Kingdom stories and
    the arts 10–15
    authenticity 46–51, 55–56
    binaries 83–84, 88–92, 100,
    125
    churches 16–17
    discipleship 52, 65–71,
    137–138
    followership 30–38, 68, 90–92
    power 1–3
    purpose 52–57, 68, 117–118
    risk 24–29, 75, 137–138
    trust 27, 72–79, 125
    typologies 39–45, 86
    wisdom and meaning 4, 58–64,
    90, 92, 102, 115, 116–119,
    121–122, 140
    identification 136–142

Kingdom of God 2–9, 12–14, 97, 125, 127–129

Kingdom of God (poem) 12–14

Kipling, Rudyard 63

Knife Angel 10–12, 136

Kocan, Peter 31–32, 38

Kostera, Monika 21, 42

Lamdin, Keith 42

Lady Bird 14–15, 20, 136

Lampel, Joseph 42

Last Judgement (Orvieto Cathedral) xviii, 83, 85–92, 97–100

Leading by Story xvii, 3, 16, 18, 43, 81, 97, 127, 140, 143

Lewin, Ann 80–82, 138

Locke, John 126

Lord's Prayer, The v, 136

McCormick Theological Seminary 41

MacCulloch, Dairmaid 45

McLellan, Dugald 86

MacMillan, Margaret 112

Mannix, Kathryn 118

Manson, T. W. 66–68

Martin, George R. R. 1

Mangham, Iain L. ix, 139

Marsh, Clive 9, 19, 84, 102–103, 137–138

Mayer, R. C. 79

Mead, Geoff 21

Michelangelo 85

Michael, St 88

Mintzberg, Henry 42

Moreau, A. Scott 55–56, 113–115, 119

Morgan, Gareth 42

Morisy, Ann 35–36

Moses 24–26

Moyise, Stephen 19

Natural Church Development (NCD) 43

Nichols, David 96

Niebuhr, H. Richard 41–43

Nietzsche, Friedrich 90

Oedipus and Creon 88

Overington, Michael 137

Perrin, Nicholas 47, 53, 80

Perronet, Edward 2

Pilgrimage 35–37, 103, 115

Piper, Tom 107

Potts, Francis 1

Power of Story to Change a Church, The 3, 81, 97

Preston, Ronald H. 93

Pritchard, John xvi

Pullman, Philip xvi, 135

Rag 'n' Bone Man (Rory Graham) 119, 131

Raphael 85

Reeve, Simon 115, 130

Remembrance Sunday 107, 118, 126

Rice, Anne xvi

Richard the Lionheart and John Lackland 88

Roberts, Vaughan S. 16, 18, 21, 40–42, 43, 45, 49, 56, 84, 97, 130, 136, 140, 143

Robson, Kirsteen x, 120

Rohr, Richard 51

Romulus and Remus 88

Rowell, Geoffrey 93

Royce, Josiah 116

Rutter, Esther 114

Sachs, William L. 95

Sadgrove, Michael 59–60

Sanders, E. P. 4–5, 7–8

Satan 88–92, 97–98

Savonarola 87

Sayers, Dorothy L. xvi

Scripts 138–139

Schoorman, D. 79

Schwarz, Hans 6, 19
Schweitzer, Albert 5–6
Shakespeare, William 63
Shape of Water, The xviii, 83,
    94–95, 140
Signorelli, Luca xviii, 83, 85–92,
    97–100
Sims, David xvii, 3, 16, 18, 21,
    40, 43, 49, 97, 127, 136, 140,
    143
Slumdog Millionaire 88
Smith, James K. A. 92, 113
Smith, Kristie 130
Social media 10, 92, 107,
    108–110
Spoelstra, Sverre 83, 89–92,
    97–98, 112
Storytelling xviii, 3–4, 9, 16–17,
    21, 66–67, 102–103, 108–110,
    116–117, 122, 124–126,
    139–140
Swinton, John 117, 124–126,
    136

Tawney, R. H. 93
Temple, William 93
Theissen, Gerd xvi, 68, 134–135
Thompson, Francis 12–14, 37,
    50, 83
Thompson, Jim 28

Thought for the Day 28, 137

Underhill, Evelyn v
Unkrich, Lee 94

Vasari 85

Walker, Simon P. 62, 74, 139
Warner, Martin 12, 14
Warwick Poppies and
    bigger stories 115–119
    ending stories 119–122
    life stories 113–115
    losing stories 124–126
    nostalgia 110–112
    social media 108–110
Washington Post 120
Watson, J. R. 2
Weber, Max 90
Weick, Karl E. 142
Welby, Justin 28
Wells, Sam 4, 16, 75, 77–78, 83,
    98–100, 112, 117–118, 125,
    127–128, 136, 142
Wesley, John 26
Willow Creek Church 41, 45
Witherington III, Ben 13, 19
World Diabetes Day 113
Wright, N. T. 52, 66–68, 74